Creel

Selected by
**Marina Warner, Adrian May,
Glyn Maxwell and Philip Terry**

Edited by
**Joshua R. Grocott, Kalyani Temmink
and Gabriela Silva-Rivero**

Wivenbooks
www.wivenhoebooks.com

ISBN 978 0 9570850 3 9

Published by Wivenhoe Bookshop,
23 High Street, Wivenhoe, Colchester CO7 9BE.

Designed by Jardine Press, Wivenhoe.

Contents

Glyn Maxwell

Foreword

After a year of teaching here, I had only glimpsed or guessed at
the breadth and depth and brilliance of writing in and around
the university, but this issue of Creel, bringing together work by
students studying at Essex, truly confirms it. Whether in verse
or prose or somewhere in the fields between the two, these writers
tell a multitude of arresting, absorbing stories. They also display
the rich rewards of Essex's open-minded, overlapping, multi-generic
approach; as poems, fragments, stories and sketches seem to
bristle with intelligence learned from other forms. In these pages,
I believe, is the early work of significant writers. You simply heard
it here first.

Abdulhay Aborsan

How Odysseus became the King of the Ghouls

Odysseus and his men were on their way back home, rowing their heavy ship as hard as they could in the middle of the Mediterranean. The sun was shining and it was hot. They were happy and enthusiastic as they had passed the trap of Scylla and the whirlpool of Charybdis. That night they were going to have a big feast to celebrate their success.

Odysseus told them, "Tonight, you, guards and oarsmen, must not drink so much you become intoxicated and fall asleep. I want you hyper-alert. I don't want to see you drunk."

Then he added, "You will be allowed to drink your portion when your shift is up."

At nightfall, the celebration started and the rest of men sang and danced happily and ate and drank so much that towards dawn they fell asleep one by one until every one of them was oblivious to the world. The officer in charge of the guards and oarsmen, prohibited from drinking like them that night, seized his chance, grabbed some wine and drank until he was so drunk that he also allowed the guards and oarsmen to drink as much as they wanted. As a result, everybody aboard was drunk and slept, leaving the ship to take its own course in the middle of the sea, and drift away aimlessly.

Late the following day, Odysseus was the first to wake up to find that all his men were asleep, bar none. He walked around the ship to inspect it. He could see the sails torn apart and the food section waterlogged by the sea water that jumped aboard as the ship lurched unattended all night. He started shouting at the sleeping soldiers until his bitter words managed to rouse some of them. He told them off fiercely until the chief of the guards came forward and said,

"I am sorry for this, sir! It is my fault and I am ready for punishment."

Odysseus was very angry but he contained himself. He ordered them to go, each to his position.

Soon night fell. Odysseus was so agitated and troubled that he could not sleep the whole night. He laid his maps on the table before him. He was trying to figure out where they were in the sea. He kept searching the sky for the stars that would help him navigate through the sea.

In the morning, the watch suddenly spied something ahead and called out,

"Land... Land... Land."

Everybody woke up and hurried to see for themselves. On the near horizon lay a large land mass, bare and rocky. They rowed in as close as they could and Odysseus ordered all his men to disembark and swim to shore and set up camp. Soon night fell; they lit a fire and sat around it when, not long after, they heard a strange sound.

"Listen!" said Odysseus.

Everybody fell silent. The sound stopped.

"I don't hear anything," said one of the soldiers.

In a while they started to hear the sound of women giggling, singing and calling, "Come, you dear ones. Come, you brave ones".

This caused confusion among the soldiers. So, Odysseus ordered that no one move; then he chose ten of his best men and led them to inspect the source of the sound. They wandered and searched around for hours but in vain. Suddenly the sound stopped and the men went back to the camp.

In the morning, they could see some trees and a body of water looming far away on the horizon. That was strange in a desert place like that. An old soldier came forward and said:

"Odysseus, let's go there, we might get some help from the inhabitants. We are almost out of water and we need food as most of ours was damaged that night."

Odysseus thought for a while. Although he was suspicious, he gave his orders to move towards the seeming oasis. Odysseus and his men walked and walked for days without reaching that place and the further they went in the desert, the hotter the weather. The old man spoke again:

"Commander, I think that we are on the shore of Al-Sahara and what we see now as trees or oasis is nothing but a mirage. We have been walking for over a week and we have not reached it. So, I suggest that we back away to the camp in case we go astray in this boiling desert and perish of hunger and thirst."

Odysseus took his advice and said they would go back to the shore in the morning. At midnight, the same sounds were heard: women giggling and singing.

"Come, you dear ones. Come, brave ones," they were saying.

"These are some jinns. Don't pay any attention to them," said the old man who was half asleep.

That night, Odysseus said he would stand guard alone all night because everyone was tired out. The men's faces were sun-burned because of walking for days in the sun and their bodies were heavy with hunger and thirst.

If you see Odysseus, alert watching at midnight, walking slowly with a shaggy beard and glittering eyes, you will easily mistake him for a wolf. He is strong-willed; the more hardships they encounter, the much more bravery and self-sacrifice he shows.

In the morning, the men were shocked to find themselves near a beautiful oasis. They could see tall, graceful women doing some chores; some were washing clothes; some others were cooking and a few boys and girls playing around them.

Odysseus gathered his men and carefully advanced towards the oasis. No sooner were they close than they saw one of the graceful women, wrapped in a beautifully coloured dress, with many women attending her.

Odysseus ordered his men to remain in their positions. Alone, he advanced towards the women.

"Greetings!" he began, "I am Odysseus, the commander of these soldiers."

"Greetings to you, sir!" the women's leader responded, smiling. "I am Calypso, and I am in charge here. You're welcome in the Sahara."

"We have lost our way. Where exactly are we?" asked Odysseus.

"In the Sahara in Libya," came the answer.

"Why don't you call your men in? You must be thirsty and tired," she said.

"But where are your men?" asked Odysseus. "I can only see boys and women."

"They went to war and never came back," replied the woman.

Then Odysseus hailed his men to come forward; they could not be much happier this time to carry out the orders instantly. After so many days in the scorching desert, the women served them with so much food and drink that they started to think they were in heaven Odysseus sent a courier after those who remained on the shore to come to the oasis.

At night, the women served wine and fruits and sang and danced for the soldiers. Everyone was filled with joy. It was such a night of pleasure and love!

In the morning, Odysseus woke up to find himself on a bed, being caressed by Calypso. When he got to his feet he could see that he was in a cage and all his men were dead; their bodies had turned blue and some of them had been beheaded; their heads stuck on posts in front of him.

Yesterday's beautiful women were now ferocious beasts, eager to suck his blood and eat him up in no time.

Calypso could get out of the cage through the metal posts as though they did not exist; she soon changed herself into a diabolical beast.

She is no ordinary human woman. She is a ghoulah, a jinniya of the foulest kind who loves death. Her face is like that of a hyena; her mouth is very long with two sharp long fangs on each side. She has short arms and sharp paws; her legs are tall and her feet look like human feet, each with five toes.

Odysseus was so puzzled that he remained speechless for a while. He just stood watching, unable to make out what was going on.

"Who are you?" asked Odysseus, breaking his silence.

"I am your love, dear," she answered craftily.

"You are an abominable beast," he shouted. "I am not your love."

The ghoulah came towards Odysseus and said:

"You were served food, drink and women," she said. "Didn't you expect to pay dearly for your pleasures?" She laughed.

"Nothing is dearer than your sweet blood and scrummy meat." Her laughing mouth moved closer to Odysseus's face.

Some of the ghouls wanted to attack him there as he stood in the cage but Calypso held them back and shouted:

"He is mine, don't come close to him. Understood?"

The ghouls dispersed, disappointed.

"Why did you not kill me like you did my men?" asked Odysseus.

"Because I want to marry you; because I love you. Plus, I don't know, there is a reason that prevented me from killing you. Well, this is not that important now as long as I want to keep you alive," she said.

Odysseus became silent. He looked at those diabolical creatures whose uncanny, disgusting voices were so terrifying. He could see them changing into nice women and back into beasts whose mouths were watering with saliva; baring their long sharp fangs as they looked towards him. Some of them were still feeding on the corpses of his men and sucking what remained of their blood thirstily.

Right before sunset, the ghoulah approached the cage and changed herself into a horrifying creature that chilled Odysseus to the marrow.

"I want you to marry me; if you refuse I will hand you over to these nice creatures who will feed on you. What do you think?" she asked and looked at Odysseus who remained silent.

"You choose me over death, right?" the ghoulah said and laughed slyly. Then she changed herself into a very charming lady. She ordered that the arrangements be made for the happy celebration.

The wedding ceremony went well; Odysseus was made a king of the ghouls. He was treated kindly by the ghouls and lived among them for years.

One day, a hoard of wolves wreaked havoc in the kingdom of the ghouls. Their attacks repeated for three days in a row; hundreds of ghouls were killed and devoured by the wolves. The ghouls became frightened to death every time they heard a wolf howling.

Odysseus knew that these diabolical creatures feared wolves more than anything else in the world. He remembered that he was once said to be a descendant of wolves; which is the reason why the ghouls did not eat him in the first place.

The ghouls were attacked over and over again by the wolves; here came the chance for Odysseus to win his freedom by repelling the wolves' attacks and proving himself strong.

The best opportunity came when, one night, the attack was so strong that the wolves killed a lot of ghouls and were about to reach the ghoulah's house where Odysseus and his ghoulah were living together. So, Odysseus grabbed his sword and swiftly went out to fight them. He stood crying aloud, his eyes were glittering,

"I, Odysseus, a descendant of the Great Wolves, order you to retreat, now! Retreat now, you coward wolves or you will rue the day that you attacked here!"

When the wolves heard his strong, wolf-like cries, they halted their attack and started to assemble around him. Then, Odysseus looked up and cried as loud as he could,

"Oh, Great Fenrir son of Loki, I ask your support!"

The wolves, upon hearing the mention of Fenrir, hurried to escape, fearing his wrath.

The aftermath of the attack was disastrous; a great number of ghouls were killed and eaten by the wolves. The rest kneeled down to Odysseus and begged for mercy.

Odysseus said "I will forgive you if you fix the ship and take me back home". The ghouls did that instantly.

Upon his departure, the ghoulah kissed Odysseus good-bye and shed lots of tears for his loss.

Patricia Borlenghi

A Tarot Sestina

1. The abbot with his monks and novice are in the monastery.
    The monarch acts hesitantly: he, old embittered King Wenceslas.
    She sits quietly, defending her honour, the blinded child
    On her chair beside the pensive Queen of Pentacles.
    The joker juggles with the conundrum of infinity.
    The audience don't care, too greedy and apathetic.

2. We are disillusioned and systematically apathetic,
    Having stopped seeking answers in the monastery.
    Yet still puzzling about the wonders of infinity
    And seeking the abdication of King Wenceslas,
    Aided and abetted by the Queen of Pentacles.
    Only one is at peace; it is the silent child.

3. Yet we cannot rest our hopes with a mere child.
    We must rouse the lazy and the apathetic,
    Guided by the Queen of Pentacles,
    Who has finally wrested power from the monastery
    Of the disillusioned and decrepit King Wenceslas.
    Now there is hope and a longing for infinity.

4. The choices are endless; there is infinity.
    Our future rests in the hands of that solitary child
    Now we are rid of the dreaded King Wenceslas.
    There are solutions, even attractive to the apathetic,
    Unrelated to that religion of the didactic monastery.
    And we cannot rely solely on the Queen of Pentacles.

5. Filled with regret, is the Queen of Pentacles.
    She gazes at the pentacle, as if at infinity,
    Longing for the peace of that monastery.
    And the only solace she has is in the child.
    She must look forward; not be so apathetic
    Or wretched, like the former King Wenceslas.

6.   On an island lives the banished King Wenceslas
       Missing his once beloved Queen of Pentacles,
       Stultified by his bored existence, and apathetic.
       So much time on his hands, like a clock striking infinity,
       He sometimes wonders what happened to the child.

*

Sudoku Tarot

Hans presents girls ungrateful beggar riding Serendipity
    nocturnally to him

Ungrateful beggar riding Serendipity nocturnally to him
    hands presents to girls

Serendipity nocturnally he Hans presents girls ungrateful
    beggar riding

Presently he hands girls ungrateful beggar nocturnally
    riding Serendipity

Girls ungrateful Serendipity presently riding nocturnally
    begging with his hands

Beggar riding nocturnally he to girls hands present
    Serendipity ungratefully

Riding girls present beggar Hans Serendipity to him
    ungratefully nocturnal

Nocturnal Serendipity ungratefully riding to him presents
    girls Hans the beggar

He Hans begs nocturnally Serendipity ungratefully rides
    girls to presents.

Mark Brayley

Madam La La's All-Stars

Madam La La's All-star Gay Drag Act
at camp Manhattan salsa bar -
all brawn and bras and cha-cha-chas;
a fast track gala *a la*
class acts, sarcasm and schnapps;
back, crack and sack wax,
spray tan and bad Wall-Mart mascara;
wham-bam thanks ma'am!

 Man, what larks?
Crank and PCP,
glad rags and handbags at dawn,
half can-can, half walk.
A grand sashay saga
as all standard snatch scrams.

Alas! Drama at Manhattan parkway:
Fag hags fall and flash gash at lads.
Brass tacks brats;
Gaydar says "Away!"

Fag hags hang back,
lads gag at haggard slags
and start a fatal fray.

Bad karma!
Madam La La calls a cab
and slams a charm
at ham glam fag hag shams.

All-star gay drag act
at camp Manhattan salsa bar -
all brawn
and bras
and cha-cha-chas.

Without U and I

There's not one place we went
that now welcomes me alone.
Each space rejects my memory
of loss, and shows less care
than anyone dares reveal,
as My Other fades beyond
what was once the sky.

We posed for photos here.
Who knows where they are now?
A gentle breeze swells the hope
that we can be once more.

Salt, seaweed and blasted sand.
Sharp tears attack the eyes and
The man, the dejected reject man,
flees the scene to go home
alone and feast on spleen.

TV Package meals fall short
of stop-gap love. No comfort
food here. Only stewed regret.
The remote control has never felt
so remote as now. And show
on show, on show, the same.
Repeat. Repeat. Repeat.
My head - a zoetrope of all we had,
as we stepped
from chance to chance
towards
the end

Spatchcocked Dignity

(From *The Egotists' Cookbook and Other Recipes for Disaster*)

Ingredients:
1 broken relationship (ideally with a hint of infidelity)
Game
Pinch of spice
Ample vodka
Tremulous dignity
1 loose binding promise
1 unscrupulous bastard
A pregnancy false alarm
3 level ladlefuls of regret

1. Cut one broken relationship, splitting it as neatly as possible down the middle.

2. Manipulate the game into an open position by breaking any backbone. Add a pinch of spice.

3. Flatten and soak the tremulous dignity with vodka until all flavours of bitterness and good judgement are nullified.

4. The dignity can then be loosely bound with a flirtatious binding promise into the spatchcocked position. This may seem awkward at first and a firm grip on resolve may be needed.

5. Prick the dignity indiscriminately with an unscrupulous bastard.

6. A false alarm for an immediate possible pregnancy adds a memorable piquant aftertaste for all.

7. Repeatedly baste with regret, one ladleful at a time at regular intervals for several years until this much revered essence takes over the majority of the favour.

8. Serve on a borrowed bed or rough carpet, depending on what is available.

Be warned, some diners find this a delicate dish and often guests will approach it with pursed lips. Don't be put off by this, the longer they spend picking over the bones, the more they will enjoy and savour the succulent flesh. The most important thing about this dish is the way in which it's served; get it right and people will talk about it for years to come.

There is nothing to be gained from handling the game gently in your preparation. Many find this a blunt and unpleasant procedure. You can also add to the flavour by introducing more than one unscrupulous bastard. This however comes with a considerable health warning: such a strong flavour can be too much for some.

*

Hot Sweet Supercilious Soufflé

(From The Egotists' Cookbook and Other Recipes for Disaster)

Ingredients:
Grease
Padding
20-40 years of a loving mother
Generous serving of hot air
Soupcon of saccharine charm (Public School or Inherent)
A dash of expensive taste
A hint of extravagance

1. Grease the assembled company for 5 to 10 minutes with a moderate amount of bawdy but authoritative small-talk to take control of the room.

2. Pad out the mixture with light and airy contrariness.

3. Mix in an overture of confidence, brought about by a lifetime of over-indulgence from a loving mother.

4. Gradually whisk in hot air to build up an over inflated substance. Whisking must be consistent, as any flaw in consistency can result in collapse.

5. Saccharine charm is vital, as without it this soufflé will simply lack taste.

6. Make a show of expensive tastes, especially those which reflect the life of someone well travelled and discerning.

7. Discard half used conversations of others, separating yolk from albumen and using appropriately.

8. Bake in a room lit by candles and (ideally) a log fire.

9. Serve immediately. Any cooling time could result in deflation.

This dish can be tricky to pull off at a dinner party with guests that you've not met before. Soufflés are notorious for collapsing and therefore I'd advise serving this dish to people who will forgive such hideous social indiscretions. If your soufflé is successful, you'll be the envy of all on the dinner party circuit. This does however come with a health warning: rabbit stew or lentil casserole friends may be lacklustre in their invitations as a result.

This dish is best served with strong dessert wine and a modicum of irony. Some social circles enjoy enhancing the postprandial patter with Peruvian marching powder. If this is the case then please ensure good quality cocaine for your guests. A good soufflé can fall foul, even at the final hurdle.

James Burch

Seven Days of Sorrow

Day One – Shock

What? Why? Huh? Sudden. Surprise. Terrible. Wide-eyed.
Struck. Lightning. Thunder. Rain. Pain. Jolt. Smashing. Crashing.
Crushing. Blow. Punch. Kicked. Falling. Numb. Dropped.
Bombshell. Bomb. Bang. Barriers. Wall. Unstable. Unbelievable.
Unexpected. Unwanted Unimaginable. Catastrophic. Pain. Burning.
Fearful. Flash. Shaking. Defensive. Pensive. Reflective. Serious.
Alive. Dead. Living. Dying. Sad. Miserable. Broken. Destroyed.
Shattered. Bollocks. Shit. Fuck. Wretched. Dirty. Dreadful. Dreary.
Grey. Void. Vortex. Vexed. Venom. Poison. Punctured. Pain.
Stabbed. Heartache. Hell. Torture. Explosion. Emotional. Escape.
Trapped. Monstrous. Momentous. Unfair. Frightened. Afraid.
Alone. Uncontrollable. Incontrovertible. Warped. Wormhole.
Vacuum. Heavy. Unsettled. Sick. Violent. Cold. Icy. Frigid.
Nervous. Unprepared. Down. Deflated. Dumped. Finished. Over.
Forever.

Day Two – Denial

A lie. Didn't happen. Won't accept. Can Fight. Will Fight. Must
Fight. Cruel joke. Very Funny. My idea. Still together. Smooth
over. Laugh again. Everything fine. Not real. Everything normal.
Reject reality. Weak moment. Probably drunk. Definitely drunk.
Mean Drunk. I'll forgive. I'll forget. Unfortunate misunderstanding.
Failed communication. We'll fix. We'll reforge. We'll mend. Bonded
hearts. Kindred spirits. Lover's tiff. Minor disagreement. Pointless
argument. Work through. Renewed optimism. Been duped. Been
tricked. A fool. How silly. We'll laugh. Laugh together. Smile
together. Love together. Still there. Never left. Testing me. Gauging
response. Should've realised. Loves me. Needs me. Wants me. She
regrets. She's ashamed. Defence mechanism. She'll reconsider. She'll
return. She'll beg. She'll apologise. I'll accept. Drink helps. Pain
eases. I know. Not over. Never over. Together again. Razor's edge.
I'm careful. I'm cautious. Waiting game. She'll break. She'll crumble.
Must persevere. Break through. Smash barriers. Her barriers.

Gut feeling. Nobody understands. Why fail? Why retreat? Why withdraw? Press on. Fight back. Show her. Prove myself. Entwined souls. Cannot break. Her loss. I'm fine. I'm good. I'm great. Never better. Embracing opportunity. Bright outlook. Wasn't wanted. Wasn't needed. Wasn't healthy. Love's hassle. Love's hard. Love's unnecessary. Love's work. Better alone.

Day 3 – Anger

She will pay. She will suffer. My anger's boundless. Fury consumes me. How dare she? How could she? Why would she? Burn the bitch. String her up. She is pain. She is torture. She is disgust. I'll get revenge. My hand shakes. My blood boils. Gods be damned. Love be damned. Pain is living. Embrace the pain. Pain fuels hatred. Hatred replaces love. She is ugly. She is unworthy. She is monstrous. Never loved her. Was using her. She will hurt. I'll hurt her. Her annoying laugh. Her mannish attributes. Her self righteousness. Her food snobbishness. She is wrong.

I loathe myself. I hate myself. I cause suffering. I'm a blight. I am lazy. Waste of space. I'm a fool. I'm a moron. I'm a cretin. I am ridiculous. I am unnecessary. I'm too proud. I'm a joke. I hurt people. I hate people. I destroy people. I'm a loser. I'm a failure. I give up. I back down. I always retreat. Not worth loving. Not worth living. I should cease. I should go. I should leave. Let myself down. Unfaithful to myself. Played with weakness. Played with fire. Burnt my hand. Hateful towards myself. Angry with myself.

The world sucks. Life is unfair. Nothing works out. Bad people succeed. Good people suffer. Love's a lie. Love doesn't exist. Love's a curse. There's no justice. Beauty always fades. Love shouldn't hurt. Love is poisoned. Pain outweighs pleasure. Fuck this shit. Life is constricting. Life is constrained. Where is freedom? Freedom is trapped. Love causes hate. Love causes anger. Love causes mistrust. Love causes depression. Love causes pain. Cannot escape anger. Cannot escape mistrust. Cannot escape depression. Cannot escape pain. Suffering defines humanity. Humanity seeks suffering. Humanity craves suffering. I hate humanity. I hate people. I hate life. I hate love.

Day 4 – Guilt

It was my fault. I am to blame. I could've done better. I could've been better. She deserved much more. I was too selfish. Never tried to understand. Didn't acknowledge her problems. Living abroad is difficult. She must be homesick. Maybe I smothered her. I asked too much. Wore my own shoes. Never tried hers on. Took her for granted. Made her feel bad. Didn't look after her. Didn't let her grow. Tried to change her. Tried to bend her. Tried to force her. Never meant to hurt. Never meant to smother. Never meant to push. Did not want this. I've let her down. I've betrayed her trust. Missed all the signs. Ignored all the signs. Were there any signs? We should have prepared. Summer was always coming. I'm racked with guilt. She is completely blameless. I brought this on. Loneliness clings to me. I let her in. Should have warned her. Could have saved us. Foresaw this months ago.

Ignored all my instincts. I should've been responsible. Maybe I took advantage. Blinded by her beauty. Brought low by love. I regret my actions. I have dishonoured myself. This is my failure. I'm prepared to self-condemn. I deserve the reproach. I've transgressed against love. I deserve the reproach. I'm prepared to self-condemn. This is my failure. I have dishonoured myself. I regret my actions. Brought low by love. Blinded by her beauty. Maybe I took advantage. I should've been responsible. Ignored all my instincts. Foresaw this months ago. Could have saved us. Should've warned her. I let her in. Loneliness clings to me. I brought this on. She is completely blameless. I'm racked with guilt. Summer was always coming. We should have prepared. Were there any signs? Ignored all the signs. Missed all the signs. I've betrayed her trust. I've let her down. Did not want this. Never meant to push. Never meant to smother. Never meant to hurt. Tried to force her. Tried to bend her. Tried to change her. Didn't let her grow. Didn't look after her. Made her feel bad. Took her for granted. Wore my own shoes. Never tried hers on. I asked too much. Maybe I smothered her. She must be homesick. Living abroad is difficult. Didn't acknowledge her problems. Never tried to understand. I was too selfish. She deserved much more. I could've been better. I could've done better. I am to blame. It was my fault.

Day 5 – Pain and sorrow

Why am I so lonely? I'm destined to be alone. My eyes are constantly glistening. I break down alarmingly regularly. Nobody can communicate with me. I am gripped by grief. Mind, body and soul, broken. Everything is burning around me. Each heartbeat's a knife wound. Vodka can numb some emotions. Nothing can numb me forever. I always remember and suffer. Each memory's tainted for now. I'll never kiss her again. I'll never make her laugh. I'll never hold her close. I'll never know her heart. She's forever lost to me. It hurts so fucking much. Shotgun hole in my heart. How can I carry on? My misery has enslaved me. I am an empty husk. I am emptied of love. I am full of sorrow. I am full of grief. I am full of pain. When can I stop feeling? I don't want to feel. Fetch me the poisonous asp. Bring me a sharpened dagger. Let the pain flow out. Love settles into a pool. Moodiness makes me bad company. I've been deserted by happiness. I've been deserted by love. I've been deserted by her. She was everything to me. Now I have nothing left. Stuck in a lamenting spiral. Wrapping myself in unbreakable chains. Cutting myself off from reality. Wrapping myself in unbreakable chains. Stuck in a lamenting spiral. Now I have nothing left. She was everything to me. I've been deserted by her. I've been deserted by love. I've been deserted by happiness. Moodiness makes me bad company. Love settle into a pool. Let the pain flow out. Bring me a sharpened dagger. Fetch me a poisonous asp. I don't want to feel. When can I stop feeling? I am full of pain. I am full of grief. I am full of sorrow. I am emptied of love. I am an empty husk. My misery has enslaved me. How can I carry on? Shotgun hole in my heart. It hurts so fucking much. She's forever lost to me. I'll never know her heart. I'll never hold her close. I'll never make her laugh. I'll never kiss her again. Each memory's tainted for now. I always remember and suffer. Nothing can numb me forever. Alcohol can for a while. Each heartbeat's a knife wound. Everything is burning around me. Mind, body and soul, broken. I am gripped by grief. Nobody can communicate with me. I break down alarmingly regularly. My eyes are constantly glistening. I am destined to be alone. Why am I so lonely?

Day 6 – Release and resolution

Today is a much brighter day. Last night brought me a resolution. I am resolved to my fate. My chest is feeling less tight. She no longer occupies my soul. She remains special, but not overwhelming. I am free of the pain. The pain is incorporated into me. My wings are ready to unfold. I am no longer in shock. I have moved past my denial. Anger won't satisfy me any longer. Won't feel guilty, not my fault. The wound'll heal, I'll be scarred. Scars are a badge of honour. I'll know I'm capable of love.

Day 7 – Return to normality

To love again is to be hurt again. All good things come to an end. It's better to have loved and lost. Now I am free to love again. Genuine security cannot be gained from others. I will return to being me. No one else will make me vulnerable. Emotions are only for the weakest people. I don't need to feel any more. I'll lock away anything that can hurt. Only through introspection can man be free. My love is transmuted into emotional oblivion. I am a phoenix reborn from fire. Goodbye new me and welcome back old.

Maybe I am not free from this?

Cristina Burduja

Sunday Apostasy

I am a piece of paper. I am green, light green. I have something written on me. It was written this morning. Written with a dull pencil, it scratched my surface. I was just another piece of paper, until there was something written on me. Now I have to wait to be read.

Monday morning:

No trace of anyone in the room. What's written on me? What am I? A message, a code, a simple stupid word? Am I something important? Wait! I hear something. Oh, it's the cleaning lady, opens the windows. "Nooooo" I scream "don't, the wind will blow me away". She can't hear, she's too busy with picking every single white dot from the floor. He hates white dots on the floor. She doesn't stay long, I wish she did. I like humans; they always look confused when they're alone. I survived. The wind was busy with the curtains. It's a nice day outside. What a day! I wish I could go for a walk in someone's pocket.

Tuesday morning:

I am woken up by the phone ringing, very loud. Why? What time is it? I hear steps. Someone is running. It's not him. Who is this lady? She doesn't even look at me. She answers: "Yes...yes...yes.... I'm sorry, but he is not home at the moment, he is out of town for a week...no...I'm sorry, he asked not to be disturbed...no, he didn't leave any message...I see...no problem...good bye". I don't like her voice. It sounds like someone who drinks at least three raw eggs every morning. She stares at the phone for a while. Walks out of the room. She smells interesting. Why didn't she look at me? I am just not important to her, but I know I am. I know I have something important on me. Something that needs to be discovered. I want to be discovered. I feel the letters pressing my surface, I know they are there. I am here. There is still time. I am sure someone will find me.

Wednesday morning:

I can't believe it took me such a long time to realise that I have a purpose. I have a purpose. I want to exist. I do exist. What a morning! Isn't this the most beautiful morning you can ever see? Look at those trees outside, how they wish for someone to touch them, to write something on them, how they wish to be acknowledged. I can't remember being a tree, but they say this is where we come from. I feel we do. We can never be sure, so I am left with just a feeling. Look at those birds! Those wings, spread as if to be able to hug the whole world. Are they really as free as they seem? I think they want me to think they are. I feel warm. I feel good. Do you hear that sound? The frogs by the lake. They sound divine. I need to talk. The pencil is always bored. All other papers don't like me anymore, they are envious. They want something written on them as well. I wish they could see how lovely this day is.

Thursday morning:

Nice, another one of those mornings when I feel like dancing. Yes, I want to dance. Oh, I wish I was a leaf, a brown and red leaf, I could dance to the ground or I can be taken anyway, folded in a journal and sent overseas, as a memory. Wait, if someone reads what's written on me, will they throw me away? I hate the trash bin, it's full of all this meaningless paper, nobody cares about. I have a meaning now, a purpose. He comes back in less than a week, he will get rid of me, I am doomed. This is just not fair. Please cleaning lady, come back, open the windows, let the wind blow me away, I want to hide under the carpet. The carpet is warm. He's clever. In need of touch he gathers all this white dots. He gets to be touched every day. He even likes dirty shoes. I don't. They ruin me. They step over everything I exist for. Dirty shoes don't care about meanings. I want to be found after years, I want to be found by someone who will care. I want to end up old. Paper is so much more beautiful when it's old. I want to be old. Oh, how I dream about becoming a book. There are so many books on this table, big books, small books, new books, old books, they all look happy. I am so close to them. This pencil, why did he choose this pencil? It's red. I guess he likes red. He also likes this desk. This desk is old. I hear it falling into the ground sometimes, slowly slowly. I like this desk. There are many things on it, they may look unorganised, but they are. Every morning he arranges everything on it. The books to the right side, pens and pencils next to them, the golden lamp on the left (so it won't shadow his hand while he writes), the phone right in the middle (it rings a lot), pieces of paper everywhere, different colours (there is something written on them too, for a very long time) and me, attached to the lamp. This is my home.

Friday morning:

Message? What a stupid piece of paper I must be, she said message, Tuesday, on the phone, she said message. Am I the letter? I am silly. How can I be a letter, I am only a piece of light green paper with something written on it. Why did he choose me, out of all these pieces of paper from his organised desk, why me? I was peaceful before, I had no worries. What is this? A kind of joke? Write something on me and then just leave, for a whole week? He is insane. I guess it's not one of my best morning moods. I'm green after all. I hate mornings. No, I don't. I hate this one. Oh, music. I hear music. I like music. Maybe he's back. Is he back? No, he left for a week. Maybe she lied. Did she? She smelled like a liar. Oh no, I am going crazy. I can't, I'm important. I have something important on me, letters, meanings. I wish someone would see me. Saturday, Sunday! Two more days. He'll be back soon. Oh, how I want to hear his voice. He has such a beautiful, masculine voice. He is a man. He is a real man. He can handle paper. He takes care of every single piece of paper. He loves paper. I feel special. I am such a lucky piece. I mean, I could've ended on another desk, in someone else's house, never touched, never paid attention to. Or, even worse, I could've ended up on some shelf, in a shop, nobody wants the paper from the shelf. It's dusty. People hate dust. Paper hates dust. It's itchy and steals your identity. We only end up appreciating dust when we're old, then it covers us in time, without dust we're never old enough. Everything is so silent. I need silence. I am here, now.

Saturday morning:

I hear voices. Something happened. What? Where? With whom? I can't understand anything. Come closer. Come closer! They are coming. Who are these people? Dirty shoes, awful! What are they doing? Why are they throwing everything around? Does he know about this? Stop it! Oh, no no, no; they are coming to the desk. Read me, I'm important. What are they looking for? A message? What message? A message from him. They say he left one. I don't remember that. He didn't. You're wrong. Stop moving things around. He won't be glad about it. What a hell is going on?

Oh, someone reads me. Finally! What is that? Why are you doing this? Stop it!

Sunday morning:

Cleaning day. Come, come, you confused cleaning lady, open those windows, I miss the sun. Open them. Thank you. What a light!
It moves all day long across the room as if trying to inspect every corner, starts with the window, then slowly, like a snake, sneaks closer to the chair, the chair smiles and becomes more comfortable, then it crawls to the desk, centimetre by centimetre, it must have all the patience in the world, then it gets to the books on the right side, the books seem to float. I start to smile. I close my eyes. I feel warm. What a great feeling.

Monday morning:

I hear music. It's the river. It's the birds. It's the desk falling into the ground. It's the light warming the grass. It's the leaves, dancing. It's everywhere. I am ash. He didn't come back.

Steph Driver

Damp

Now the pendulum begins oscillating
    Swinging forward
          Back
          again Swing forward
          The pendulum expends energy
          Swinging to and fro ever on
          Apes perpetual motion
          But not now
          A
      To n Fro
    Leaving energy
   Behind swinging
    slower, slower
     Swinging
        in
          the
          slowing
          periodic
          motions
          every
          to
        n
       fro
      slow
      ever
      fro

        ,

        I
        go
        on
        or
        I

        d
        i
        e

        .

Disabled

```
              CAN'T
           don't say
          CAN'T to me
          I CAN and I
          do.  I take
           the pills
            and am
             like
             many
             many
             well
   Not       'normal' people
   many      Am I different?
   other     A diabetic must
   souls     take
   don't     some
   have      pills
   some-     so must I.  Does not
   thing     mean that I'm inferior
 wrong.      or to be pitied.  I'm a
 We're        person too.  I think. I
 valid                    feel. I
 human                 love an     d
 beings                  I cry t oo.
 living              To   My blood
  in our            live  spills
   unique           exist    too
    ways &          amidst
    without        'normal'
     handicap.      handicap.
        Disabled, not broken
           don't pity us.
              EQUAL
```

Lydia Graystone

Pictures of Lily

Sharon

Lily Kalinowski didn't walk down the aisle until she was thirty-seven, and you'd have thought she'd have given up trying by then, but apparently it's never too late to sink your claws into a rich doctor. We were all pretty embarrassed on her behalf, but she was getting married and we wanted to show our support. That was five years ago now. And I say she walked down the aisle, but she didn't, not even at her own wedding, because the silly cow got married in a field. We got the invitation and I said to Dave, *this is just another of her silly jokes*, because who gets married in a field? I wore my best heels and they were absolutely ruined.

Well, she walked down the field, and I couldn't believe it. Her hair. It looked exactly the same as it used to do in the 80s, and I remembered all those afternoons after school when we would sing and dance around to Janet Jackson in her room, and I would long to reach out and touch it. But how embarrassing, to walk around on your own wedding day in 2006 with a big old crimped brown nest on top of your head. And then just when I thought things couldn't get any more humiliating, she ripped it off! The whole thing was a wig. She was bald underneath, and her head looked so awful poking out of the top of that white dress, shiny and pale and smooth as a naked mole rat. Her husband must have been dying inside.

In the end she tossed it, like a horrible hairy bouquet – because of course, she couldn't have flowers like everyone else does – and all the women scrambled in the mud like pigs, trying to catch it. I stayed well out of it. I was hardly about to ruin my dress for a dirty, matted old wig.

Doug

Lily Lily Lily my therapist told me to try this stream of consciousness writing where you don't use any full stops and you just write the first thing that comes into your head but I don't know how much good it's going to do me, because it's not going to bring you back – besides he also told me to remember you before the cancer but that doesn't work because then I miss out on seven years of memories with you, like that beach party in 2009 when you stamped on all my sandcastles just like when we were kids, or the time you phoned me up breathless to tell me you'd just met Piers Morgan and you'd called him a wanker, or especially your wedding day, because I couldn't believe that after years of going out once with all my mates and then getting bored of them you'd found someone who could keep you interested – but on your wedding day it really was like I was remembering you before the cancer; you had that dodgy permed wig on, and you looked just liked you used to every morning before school when you hogged the bathroom mirror to do your hair and put our makeup on so I couldn't shave and I grew that stupid wispy beard – but then you threw the wig away and you'd shaved your head, and you came up to me later to tell me you were finally starting chemo and said *Aren't you proud of me? Totally unshallow on my part* and I was so drunk I promised to save up to buy you one of Cher's actual stage wigs, and I finally got enough money together this year and I ordered it but it never did arrive, and now I worry that I made you think I thought you looked ugly with a shaved head and that you ought to cover it up, but it just scared me because my little sister suddenly looked like the cancer was written all over her, but now I look at your wedding photos and I know it's corny but you've never looked more beautiful.

Nina

Lily and I had known each other since we were four and our mothers made conversation as they towered over us in the playground, so I wasn't too surprised when she asked me to be a bridesmaid at her wedding. The real surprise was that she was getting married at all. Usually when I saw Lily she'd be bright, bouncy and resolutely not tied down to anyone; she'd tell me she was learning to figure skate or recovering from getting drunk with the inhabitants of her local retirement home or... well, there was no 'usually' about it, except for the feelings of envy that always overwhelmed me. She even made her illness look appealing. *Neens, I had a breast exam today. It was dead sexy. The doctor found a lump, but we're having dinner on Saturday!*

Two years later and she and her doctor are getting married in a field, and she's absolutely glowing. I'm smiling at her, feeling just as drawn to her as I did when we were little, when I would stare enviously at her hazel eyes and golden skin and long chestnut hair, intensely conscious of my freckles and gappy teeth and sullen, pasty little face. I married ten years before she did, and I have my husband and my children and my health (and I thank God for these blessings every day) but I still can't quash the feeling that she's the one who's living the fairytale, or overcome my awe of her beauty and vibrancy quite enough to call her my best friend.

She rips off the wig and I'm speechless. Without it her skin seems so much whiter, her eyes so much larger, and when she throws it into the air I fight tooth and nail to catch the darn thing because it's a little piece of her, and when I succeed it perches atop my drunken head for ten delirious minutes, until I see her dancing to Eternal Flame with her new husband. She's leaning into him looking just as luminous and perfect as ever and his hands are gently stroking the back of her bald head, and I slowly take off the wig and put it down on the grass.

Mike and Vanessa

We were so surprised when Lily said she was getting married.

Well, she'd always said she didn't want to when she was a little girl, and we just assumed she'd change her mind. Most people do. But she never did, did she, Mike?

She never did. Not even at thirty, which, if you recall, was the age you were when I persuaded you to give it a go.

Not that we minded! She was always so independent. And she seemed so happy.

Oh yes, always in good spirits.

Even after the diagnosis...

The diagnosis was how she met Pat, after all. Good chap, Pat.

Oh, Pat's nice, isn't he?

Damn good chap.

And the wedding was lovely, wasn't it? She said she wanted it in a field and I knew she'd get what she wanted. She always does.

Always did. Even when she was a toddler.

Oh, she was a gorgeous toddler. And she looked so beautiful in her dress. That perm of hers, it was like going back in time! Do you remember it? When she was sixteen?

Mmm. Always messing around with her ruddy hair, wasn't she?

Always doing something. She was obsessed! That's why I couldn't believe it at the wedding – she'd shaved it all off!

Shaved it all off. Completely gone. I used to tease her about that – tell her I was fed up with her messing around with it, and she should get a number two shave like me. And she'd go Eurghh, DAAAAD! Yuck, no way!

She was a moody so-and-so, wasn't she?

From the day she turned thirteen.

But it didn't last.

It was over after a few years. The hair lasted though. Twenty years later, and she finally shaves it!

Oh, Mike. That was for the chemo. I didn't like to look at her.

Yes, dear, I know it was for the chemo. But once she'd thrown that hairpiece away I thought she looked lovely. And when we had our little dance at the wedding, do you know what I said to her?

Yes, dear.

I told her I'd always thought she would have a beautifully shaped head, and now I knew for sure.

Patrick

People laugh about the way Lily and I met because it sounds like a dirty movie. But it wasn't the breast exam that made me ask her out; of course it wasn't. It was because even though I'd been performing breast exams for about ten years, I was far more nervous than she was. She kept cracking these terrible jokes, even after I told her I found the lump – *Are you sure it isn't just a cheese football? I think I dropped one down my top earlier* – and it felt strangely intimate, as though I were already her husband and she was trying to comfort me.

When we did marry two years later everything was hyper-real. We were in a field and she was walking towards me with her father on her arm and the evening smelled like wet grass and summer rain.

Typical Lily refused the wedding march just like she refused a church and a traditionally ordained reverend, and walked up the non-aisle to Kate Bush's Wuthering Heights. And I was looking at her in that magnificent permed wig feeling like I was meeting her twenty years before I did.

We were married, and when I held her and kissed her, her skin was soft as ever, and she tasted like a sausage sandwich. When she pulled her wig off and threw it into the sea of women before her, I saw a tiny grease stain on the bodice of her white gown, which had previously been hidden by a lock of crimped brown hair. She'd already been at the buffet, but I was the only one close enough to notice that she'd dribbled on her wedding gown, and I smiled.

Later on, when we were swaying to the strains of the Bangles, I stroked her smooth, bald head, buried my face in her neck and inhaled. Jasmine and honeysuckle, with just the slightest hint of pork.

Helen

I go to a lot of weddings, and this was a lot like the others. The bride had tried to be different, just like they all do. Barefoot in a field, with an internet-ordained registrar, a picnic buffet, and a selection of dire 80s music blaring out of a tinny old iPod? Half-arsed. I went to a druid wedding once – long white robes, chanting, bonfire, midsummer night, the works. Now that was interesting to shoot. But if there's one thing I've learned from working weddings, it's that what the bride says goes.

So I didn't mention the fact that the registrar she'd chosen wouldn't actually give her a legally binding marriage, and I didn't say a word when I saw her in that awful wig, though I don't know who she thought she was kidding with it. She'd clearly got it from a joke shop for a tenner. I was relieved when she chucked it to her bridesmaids in lieu of a bouquet – I got a great shot of it whirling through the sky, one for the arty, non-wedding portfolio.

Later, when I was getting a few shots of the bald bride on her own (been there, done that – Hare Krishna weddings are a blast) I asked if it had been a symbolic gesture. You know, casting aside of the shallow, sexist fixation upon female hair in order to embrace a deeper, more spiritual side.

Everything's a symbolic gesture when you've got cancer, she said, grinning. *I just thought it would be funny.*

Joshua R. Grocott

A Quick One

"Don't be daft."
He said to her
As she was brushing her hair.
She looked at him, in the mirror,
'Cause he were standing there
[Points behind shoulder].

"How am I being daft?"
She said to him
And fixed him with her sharpest frown.
He shuffled slightly,
Feeling rightly foolish,
Dressed in her pink dressing gown.

 "I didn't mean nothing by it."
He stammered,
After all, he were quite enamoured
With the girl who sat before him
[Points to where she sits]
Giving him a nasty look.
Just three words spoke out of turn
Was all it ever took,
But still, he'll never learn.

Slowly and with practiced malice,
She popped her hairbrush in a chalice
That sat upon her dressing table.
He couldn't move, he wasn't able,
As she swivelled round to face him.

"Then what exactly did you mean?"
She sounded a little like the Queen
As though she had minions,
Yet unseen,
Waiting to stab him in the spleen
When he failed
To give the right answer.

Then with the grace of a ballet dancer,
He saw a way to put one past her:
He fumbled with the knot,
Whipped off the silky gown
(Quick as the proverbial shot)
And prostrated himself before her.

"Oh my god! What are you wearing?"
She laughed at him,
The tension tearing.
'Cause as his arse stuck in the air,
Amongst bum-fluff and pubic hair,
She spied her frilly g-string.

"And you called me daft?"
She laughed again.
He grinned back, by her feet,
Looking slightly insane.
The argument had been diverted,
And instead of looking quite perverted,
He earned himself a quickie.

The moral of the tale is this,
My friends;
If you ever need to make amends,
Before an argument begins
Or before you're bollocked
For your sins...

If (by some amazing stroke of luck)
When you hear your partner shouting
"Fuck!"
You happen to be wearing something
Pink and frilly,
You may as well show her
'Cause (either way)
You will look silly.

GINESIS:
THE ORIGIN OF THE SPECIOUS

The three wise drunken gargoyles touched down on savage land,

There they met a savage folk, whose skills they did demand.

The wisest of the savage men took the gargoyles' severed parts.

He left his kindred on the mount, to end what he did start.

The savages took their sleeping foe and trapped them in a pot.

The pot was used to distil gin, so the men distilled the lot!

When the Sun had fully set, the gargoyles woke in panic; they had the wisdom of the gods, but not the strength to back it!

The moon shone as the gargoyles gurgled, fire licked and cauldron burbled, stewing the only brew.

The wise man's wife took her husband's meat, and prepared a meal for them both to eat.

She crushed the eyes into their cups; upon the ears and tongue the pair did sup.

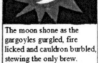

The gods' Nectar steamed from the gargoyles' veins, condensing through the still's vapour drains, and settled in a jug; from which each savage took a lug.

The man and wife consumed but trace amounts and so received just vague accounts, yet still they were too much.

The other folk drank a higher proof; they were never meant to know such sooth and, lo, their heads exploded!

So Adam returned to the hill. He took a hammer to the still, then turned and walked away.

The gargoyles, deprived of sacred Nectars, were left to stand as stony spectres;

Reminding us of the harm that's done, when we say:
"Can't hurt to have just one!"

That Will Bring Us Back To –

Doe: a deer, a female deer, which can also be called a cow or hind.
Ray: a pianist, last name Charles.
Me: the personal pronoun or object form of "I".
Far: an unspecified measurement of relative distance.
So: a useful word that can be an adverb, adjective, interjection and a noun (in music).
La: the sixth note of the major scale, or "the" in French and Spanish.
Tee: a stand used to support a stationary ball in games like golf or tee-ball.

That will bring us back to –

Doe: a rabbit, a female rabbit, also the female of numerous other species.
Ray: an idealised narrow beam of light (which physicists believe can travel as a wave or as particles, but rarely as "drops").
Me: Myself and I.
Far: is not something that is near.
Sow: is the verb that describes planting seeds. Not to be confused with "sewing" in textiles, or the noun "sow" which brings us back to "doe" in some respects; being a female aardvark, anteater or armadillo (to name but a few).
La: a genus of moths of in the Crambidae family, including only four species that all have "punning" names (La benepunctalis - for the 1919 La Benepunctalis Hampson Encyclopaedia of Life, La cerveza- for the alcoholic beverage, La cucaracha - for the traditional Spanish folk corrido, and La paloma - which is a female given name that might also bring us back to doe again, if we didn't have to stop for tea first).
T: describes the shape of my shirt and, coincidentally, tea is what caused the stains down the front of it.

That will bring us back to –

(Incidentally; the more common spelling of the syllables that make up the Latin version of the major scale could lead to a totally different mnemonic learning device, to that employed in the Rodgers and Hammerstein score).

Do: unto others (etc).
Re: the last email I sent you...
Mi: the Roman numeral 1001.
Fa: meaning sweet FA in British idiom (but is the fourth note of the major scale in sol-fa musical notation).
Sol: the Sun in Latin based languages, a Roman sun god and a Norse sun goddess, as well as a cerveza which might more accurately be known a drop of golden sun (because it tastes like burning).
La: what you sing when you don't know the words.
Si: the chemical symbol for silicon. ("Si" is usually replaced by "Ti" in tonic sol-fa though).

That will bring us back to –
Grab your partner by the hands and do-si-do!

Leanne Haynes

Miss B.

Miss B. was in no hurry to make her way to
the train station this morning. It was a welcome
relief, since this frantic monotony was no good

for her sensitive (but troubled) soul. For her,
the train station was both banal and brilliant,
a love-hate relationship that plagued her like the

insects of the night, which try and talk to her when
she is weary and wanting to forget: "Admirable
though," she thought out loud, as she remembered the

night-flyers that clinked against the table lamp. "Look
at them as they dash into another world, from
the closed-lids of the night to the bright whites of my

fake day." Yes, it was bright white, the light that tempted
her this morning, to leave the deepest caverns
of her dreams behind. Oh, but this is not to say

that Miss B. wanted to leave this Freudian frenzy,
no, for it was these nocturnal journeys that gave
her sleepy Zzzzzz the courage to metamorphose

into lives. By day, she lived the lives of others.
A footstool for their fears and fantasies. She
was there as another self, a healing woman,

or so she was told. By nightfall, she used what bad
she could to re-create and make their histories
their own. Miss B. writes lives. It dawned upon her

that the sun was now high, yoked and sized with the lies
and secrets that only it can see from way up
there. She drank down her coffee (customary to her

day) and surfed along with the stimulant in her
bloodstream. She grabbed the flowers, which were all prepared
and waiting to go (she always bought the flowers

herself), pulled the door shut and the door knocker tapped
away as if it was saying goodbye. She walked
towards the train station, both banal and brilliant.

Island Episodes

Episode One,
The sea was the sea.
The harbour was now still and the
boats were sleeping.
The anchor's crabbed claw burrowed deep
hermitting in the mud that was naked
because the tide had left for a while.

Episode Two,
The crab slowly lifts his head,
sieves the sand in
fine inspection –
moves mastered by agility.
He notices my curiosity,
pen poised, edging towards
blank page-
He fast retreats.
Back to the hole from which it came.

Episode Three,
The thud of an orange foot.
It was the Gull, the bully of the bird world.
With each waxed foot,
trod on the sludge,
then lifted wings spread,
take him to the hull.
Neck jolts forward
to scream a dying scream,
carries his mucky body
to survey the horizon.

Episode Four,
The island noises fill my ears,
like a conch shell and the murmur
of the sea. The iguana on a rock,
centuries stuck,
reminds us
of beginnings.

Oliver King

A Step-by-Step Guide to Recycling Your Unwanted Household Items

She is reading from the pamphlet, out loud in her holier-than-thou voice, and it is doing my head in.

We believe that looking after our planet is a difficult task but a necessary one. We have a vision for a cleaner, healthier county. That vision requires the combined and determined work of each and every one of us. We hope you'll share our vision.

In my far vision, the sky above the tip is finally clearing. The clouds have all been folded back on themselves and are doubled up and tall like stacks of storage boxes, clouds packed inside clouds to save space in the sky. In my near vision, the windscreen is chipped and smeared and, in a smudge, the black, gritty insides of a ladybird are all laid out, drying and losing colour in the sun. Ronnie sits in the passenger seat in her green cotton dress, with one hand on her stomach and the other holding the instruction pamphlet, and chews an indigestion tablet and talks at the same time.

The signs say: 'cars and single-axle trailers', 'Permit needed for vans', pickups/flatbeds' double-axle trailers', 'No commercial vehicles', 'No commercial waste'. As we go in under the low-slung height restriction bar, the trailer rattles and its contents answer loudly and I can feel it bounce and drag on the back of the Astra. The concrete road curves around and away and into sunlight and off to the skips and containers and hoppers, each a different colour. We pass endless signage, each reflecting sun – warnings, precautions; 'for more information call our hotline', 'to apply for permits visit our website'.

Some items can be put out with your household waste on your normal kerbside collection day. See page eleven. There are also some items which we cannot put into the landfill or recycle. These items are toxic and there are strict government regulations – aitch-four-five-b-blah-blah-blah - concerning their disposal. See page twenty-four.

"Jesus Christ, will you shut up? I'm not fucking five!"

She looks up. "You won't talk to me like that when the baby comes."

"Oh you wanna bet? If you keep nattering away like that, don't you worry, I'll say whatever I want, all right?"

She shakes her head. "Fine, me too."

We go round the curve, five miles an hour, to the first available parking space, and I pull in, the trailer awkwardly following, sticking out. In front of us is a big black roll-on roll-off skip, ten feet tall, with metal stairs up the side. The sign on the ro-ro says: 'Non-recyclable waste – no rubble, no hardcore, no soil – landfill'.

"Oh," Ronnie says.

"Oh what?"

Can I recycle old photographic film, negatives and photos? Currently we do not offer recycling of old film or photographic stock and these must be disposed of in the black skip. If you need to dispose of nitrate film please see page twenty-four.

"So, wait, so we could have just binned them?"

Ronnie shrugs. "Hmm."

"This black skip?"

"I think so."

"Fucking hell." I snap off the ignition, my seatbelt whips across me and smacks the steering wheel. I yank on the door handle and get out. When I look back, Ronnie is staring at me. Her hair is done up in an emergency bun, a pencil through it to keep it steady, rubber end up. "So are you going to give me a hand or what?"

"If I get out, the smell is going to make me sick. I told you before we left."

"Okay, whatever." I slam the door. And now it is hot summer. The sun has stirred the air and has lifted up and arranged all the smells of the recycling centre before me, concrete, tyres, diesel, hot metal, and we are on the hard shoulder on our way to Bournemouth and Dad has the bonnet up and Mum is biting her nails. I'm eating quartered cheese sandwiches from the coolbox and Judith is telling Mum it'll be okay and that Dad knows everything there is to know about engines. And it is so hot the cheese in the sandwiches is wilted and rubbery. Mum conscripts a smile. Dad swears. And it is so hot the car, a Skoda back when people made jokes about them, is more vapour than solid and the July heat hangs heavily in the space between Mum, Judith and me, while Dad is just an ambiguity in the swaying air, his gentle swearing coming to us like a language from the past, recognisably our own.

"All right, mate? Need a hand?"

"Nah, no worries, mate, cheers."

The man in his steelies and safety orange hi-vis nods and walks away. And, yes, now, the smell of the tip is developing its complexities. And, yes, walking down the road on bin day is enough to make Ronnie bend over into the gutter and puke. Seagulls circle and shriek and crosshatch the sky, a sparse matrix of white and grey out over the landfill. The first box in the trailer is the lightest and it comes up and out in my hands as if eager to be lifted. Negatives, it says on the side of the box, in Ronnie's handwriting. Recycle, save the world. Whatever Ronnie. The metal stairs shake and chime as I climb them. Ladybirds cluster on the handrails, communing on the silvery rivets. The box weighs little, then nothing. The negative strips, hundreds, hundreds, flutter down into the vast ro-ro and are gone in the gaps between other people's rubbish.

Tap tap on Ronnie's window.

"What about videos? And cassette tapes?"

Ronnie shakes the pamphlet, gives a bit of a frown. "Black skip."

"You're having a fucking laugh."

"Sorry."

My memories of holidays in Hastings are orange-stained and blurred by years, sweating through evenings in the caravan, cooled by Calippos and 99 Flakes, back when they had colours added, and preservatives. I remember punching Judith, one evening, while we were playing at the swings in the caravan park, and she fell into the woodchips. So she ran crying to Mum and Dad, of course, and I ran to the sea wall and sat there and watched the sunset until Dad found me. Last month, when I had asked her if she wanted to deal with the stuff from Dad's house, she had said definitely not. I thought she was going to complain about not having enough room to take anything and I had planned to snap back that she and Simon had far more space in their home than Ronnie and I did. But she didn't mention space, just said she couldn't do it. I'd snapped at her anyway and told her how unfair it was that my flat was filled with this crap, floor to ceiling, and I was being saddled with the job of sorting and tossing all that shit. She wasn't going to lift a finger, she didn't care, some daughter she was. "I wouldn't be able to throw any of it away," she had said, and hung up.

Tap tap.

"Rugs?"

"Erm, no, hold on, carpets, rugs, rugs, yeah, rugs, yeah, recyclable." Ronnie jerks her thumb towards the other skips. "Blue."

"Thank fuck."

The blue skip is across the road, much smaller than the black, and there is already a rolled up rug or carpet visible over the edge, standing on its end, cigar-like. Dad's rug is about six by eight, well-trodden, and, when it is rolled and bound with twine and resting on my shoulder, it is light enough to be easily hurried across the road. There are no stairs here, one bounce, two bounces, the end of the rug balances on the edge of the skip, then it's sliding over, then I shove it all in, all in one go. The rug on which we sat, cross-legged, and watched Saturday morning cartoons in the living room and spilled drinks, on which we opened Christmas presents in front of the gas fire, on which I knelt and messed about while a staticy and much-rewound foreign porn film played on the video recorder, on which Judith did her dance practices when they moved it to her bedroom, and the rug on which they found Dad lying face down, his dressing gown fallen open, Dad naked underneath. It vanishes down inside the skip with a soft report that echoes in the steel. There are ladybirds crawling along the rim of the skip, aimlessly. They are level with my eyes and I am not quite tall enough to see over them, over the rim.

Tap tap.

Ronnie is watching a seven-spotted ladybird walking in circles on the window.

"TV," I say, wiping my face with my sleeve.

She nods and points to a shipping container at the far end of the tip. "That red one, all the way over there. Do you wanna take the car round?"

"No. No, I'll just carry it."

"You sure?"

"Yeah, why not?"

"It weighs a ton."

I was born in the summer of '76 and one of Mum's favourite stories was that ladybirds were trying to get in through the windows in the maternity ward, hundreds of them. The nurses shut and locked the windows and the ladybirds crowded all around the panes like squirming orange caulking. Because the ladybirds bit. And so the mothers had boiled. Mum told it well and it always managed to make people laugh or tut in disgust, and if Dad was ever there he would roll his eyes and leave the room. She had never got the chance to tell it to Ronnie, and I have never thought to, because even though I guess it involves me in a small way, it isn't my story to tell. It died with Mum and that's okay because I wouldn't be able to tell it well enough to own it.

"S'all right. I'll manage."

"Darrell."

"Don't you dare," I tell her as she pops open her door. She closes it.

It is an old cathode ray tube and very heavy. Lifting it is like lifting it and everything that came before it. How could any single thing weigh this much? There are no good handholds in the TV's moulded back, so I have to make do with gripping on the bottom. The sharp metal edges tear my fingers, resist me. I know Ronnie is watching as I stumble, blindly, in the general direction of the shipping container. 'Toshiba', the back of the TV says, the sticker peeling. The aerial socket stares at me.

"Need a hand?"

The man in the hi-vis doesn't wait for an answer and takes one end of the TV from me.

"Cheers," I say.

"Jesus, this is a big'un. Bloody hell. Old one an' all. Does it still work?"

"No idea, mate. Hasn't been turned on for years, far as I know."

As we reach the shipping container and crab-walk through the open end into darkness, the sun shrinks to just heat and a witness to shifting particles of dust. As we place the TV on the metal floor, I glance back through the open door, at a sky that now clearly can't remember clouds, at the evaporating puddles on the concrete which are like mysteries left to us from a previous age. The ladybird that crawls from the wood-grained plastic veneer of the TV onto my hand seems less an insect than a refugee. Don't leave me here. Save me. I wonder if it will bite.

Looking at the TV, I see a faint light reflected there and an image of me, tiny in the centre of the empty screen, tiny and dust-covered and surrounded all about by grey glass.

Emma Kittle

The Hide

The sharp wind did not hinder Miles' journey along the edge of the reservoir, and from one hide to another. To his right the gentle slopes of patchwork fields were haphazardly joined with almost invisible seams. He could see, just below the peak of the hill, the tip of the new centre. They were still building, still going ahead after all his protestations that the views, the birds, would not be the same as those from the old hides.

As he walked on to the William James hide, his favourite, he could see the abhorrent skeletal structure looming over the edge of the lake.

Inside he took his place on the low bench, unhinging, and gently opening the narrow window onto the world. He got up and stood back in the small dark room which was no bigger than two metres square. And again, mesmerised by the slit of beauty which was not unlike a painting in a fine art gallery, he felt the heart murmur that he had felt every day since they'd planned – well Maria had planned and he'd constructed – the hides, the woodland walk and the whole place in fact.

When he left the hide as he had found it, he looked up, as he always did, at the rust-tinged maple trees still illuminating the dull landscape.

Today, when he reached Wyke hide, he did not unlatch the door, he did not look for anything untoward, and he did not enter. Instead he made sure that he was silent on approach, treading lightly and carefully and pausing a few yards from the hide to listen. On hearing nothing he moved another step forward and twisted his body so that his ear rested against the crack of the door. Now all he could hear was muffled scratching. Miles smiled.

*

Anne Brown unlocked her office that morning and saw on the calendar above her desk one of the green site visit stickers. Wincham reservoir. She sighed and turned on her computer. The new Pmail diary popped up. She still hadn't adapted to using the latest technology.

The phone rang, before she had had a chance to get her coffee. She snatched the handset from the receiver. 'Anne Brown,' she said.

'Oh hello,' said a voice. 'I'm phoning about the housing.'

'I'm afraid there's a lot of housing.' Anne was going to have to speak to Debbie about stopping the public access to her direct line.

'Oh,' said the voice. 'I need a house near the school. We've been given one too far away.' For God's sake she thought. Not this again. The woman with the disabled son. 'Is that Mrs. Wade?' She looked back to her computer and began to scroll her inbox.

'Yes it is,' said Mrs. Wade.

'Then I have told you that the only plot available is 127. They were allocated early on and there is no chance now of changing.' All those black unread Pmail diary introductory messages and one from her friend Amanda.

'But I know the man they say got the house near the school, number 110, and he doesn't need it, not like we do.'

'Mrs. Wade. The plots have been allocated. There isn't anything that can be done about it. Now if there's nothing else, I'm very busy.' She opened Amanda's message and went to get her coffee from the kitchen.

*

When Miles approached the visitor centre he saw the beige mini cooper in the car park. He thrust back his shoulders and made sure that his sweater was still tucked neatly into his jeans. He entered the shop-cum-cafe briskly, interrupting the intense chat that Brian was having with the woman from the council.

'Hello, Miles. This is Anne Brown – she's come to have a look around.' Miles knew very well what she was here for; Brian had, of course, warned him of the impending meeting and everything that it meant for them.

He looked her up and down, she did not fit here with her pointed red shoes; not a birder or a twitcher, or part of one of the families that sometimes came. Maria had said that it was good for children to get close to nature, to the birds. What would happen in the future if the families did not come now? But Miles could not care less about children or their families or the future any more. Not since she'd gone.

His mouth did not force a smile, but he nodded in Anne's direction and as she followed him out of the building he gazed only ahead. So he did not see Brian carefully removing the binoculars from the glass cabinet.

As they moved silently along the walkway, through the woods, Anne commented on the dens he had created from logs. 'Did you make them?' She said.

He grunted.

She thought that the attempts at a woodland campfire looked a bit scrappy. Hurrying along behind him, she noticed the small lakes surrounded by bent and bulging and torn net fencing. When they came out into the open and she saw the hills surrounding the reservoir, she found them to be threadbare. It was a shame about the hundreds of small trees they'd planted, but then they should have sought permission early on.

When they arrived at William James hide he opened the door, unlatched the windows and left her standing in the wooden box. When she scurried out after him, he said, 'Did you see? Did you see what you will be drowning with your plans?'

'I saw. I know. It's nice here. But not as nice as it will be.'

'I know what you're trying to do,' he said. 'You'll destroy everything.'

'No. We won't be destroying anything. We'll be improving.' They were at the second hide now and he did the same as he had in the first.

'Did you see?' He looked her in the eye, willing her to understand.

'Yes. And do you know what you'll be able to see from the new centre?' Miles knew it was no use.

'I know what you want to do, but I'm not moving.' They wanted his lodge, the home they'd created together; where he and Maria had quietly nurtured the cassowaries until the day she left without a word. He turned and strode toward the final hide. This one was really going to show her.

Her stomach tightened and then catapulted her voice from her mouth. 'You have been offered a good deal, Mr Webb, the new houses are much to be desired and yours, plot 110, is in the best position.'

When he continued to ignore her she said, 'And you do know that there will be a site manager position available at the new school?' As she stumbled after him, she began to open her bag to get out the plans, but he just said, 'Puh'.

'Have any other house you like?' She was catching him up again. 'Mr Webb. You know that we cannot maintain the water levels as they are, that the water companies have taken enough already and what with the new housing, the further reduction in the levels will mean that many of your birds won't have the right environment to survive here anyway.

He had already heard this argument. He knew by now that he would not convince her. And Brian admitting his fear of entrapment had certainly given him food for thought. Poor Brian. How foolish he was. Miles had to purse his lips now to prevent a smile.

Anne was preoccupied by her fight, and the knotted fishing baskets piled against the side of the hide they had approached. Before she knew it, he had stopped and she walked into the back of him. She stepped quickly to his side, treading too heavily on one foot, losing her balance and grabbing one of the cages at the top of the pile for support. Fortunately they were heavy, and knitted together by the ends of the ridged ropes that formed the bars. She smoothed down her woollen coat and took a deep breath.

When he opened the door to Wyke hide she walked in voluntarily. When he slammed the door behind her she was momentarily startled. When the birds in their shock flapped and screeched and scratched she fell backwards trying to protect her face with her hand.

After what seemed like long enough, he opened the door and said, 'Do you see now?'

*

Anne cowered in the corner with her head wrapped in her arms. When he opened the door she shuffled towards the light. When he said, 'Do you see now?' and laughed, she inched down the slope veiling her eyes, and as she lowered her arms they felt heavy.

Her nose ached and her legs could not stretch from a squat. She felt the urge to push. The strength of her thrust was such that she propelled herself through the cold wind swooping into the sky as though she were swimming, sweeping back the water in giant breast strokes. Her arms were so powerful that she let her legs dangle behind her, delighting in their weightlessness. She swooped high. High up to the sky and then stopped.

She hovered. And she sang. The song swept through every inch of her; a sherbet tingling in her claws, a whirling hot lava in her rotund belly, shooting lightening forks to the tips of her wings. When it left her, the pinnacle of her experience was its perfect pitch.

Miles Webb stood outside Wyke hide as his precious birds escaped, squeaking and squawking and spluttering, and stared up at the creature that hovered above him. The moment of revenge had certainly created an unexpected result.

The creature sang. And then she dived. As fast as a diver from the top board she hurtled towards him. She saw his eyes, wide and wild, and then shielded by the crook of his elbow.

*

The local news said that the caretaker of the reservoir had been attacked by his own birds. Council worker Anne Rose Brown had disappeared on the very same day visiting the site. Although her red jacket and shoes and samples of her blood had been identified, no body had been found.

Neither had a close relative that could indicate their preferences otherwise so a memorial to them both would be placed in the new lake. The one that would flood the old, and become the centre of a new complex. A viewing tower would be ideally positioned for viewing the small island that would hold the memorial plaque, in the very same spot that Wyke hide now stood.

The lake would provide drinking water for the growing towns of Bide and Wincham, where a twenty per cent population growth was predicted and which would be accommodated by the many family homes to be built around the reservoir. And of course, the creation of which would provide jobs and educational experiences for the whole community.

*

But before they came to proceed with the next stage of the expansion works the council were forced to stop.

A rare bird, and then another, as yet unidentified, had been spotted. They perched on the top of Wyke hide and swooped back and forth between the maple trees. They had been observed for a while and rarely sung, but when they did their song was almost melancholic.

And then, some others, blue-necked and at once beautiful and grotesque, were seen trotting across the fields as if they had been there all their lives.

Of course, the twitchers started arriving in droves and the café was full for the first time. Brian, encouraged by the effects of his letter to the council, and bemused by the latest developments, started to rebuild the woodland camps. And he decided, that after a lick of paint, he would move into the woodland lodge himself.

Matthew L. Kroll

(In a sad sorry room...)

In a sad sorry room
with a tiny twin bed
I with nothing to do
no friends no school no job
    We stayed up all night and slept all day
     You never went to class.

In a blurred anecdote
a smoldering cigarette lit the trash
the burning plastic smell –
        then we saw a flame
peak out from behind crumpled paper
We said "oh shit" simultaneously
the way movie duos do.

In reaction succinct
You leapt up and in a hushed shout
instructed me: fetch a pillow
open the windows
turn on the fan
get water
       ...a hissed series of do's.

In one flush movement
You doused the flame
swung two-handedly the pillow
fanning thick smoke toward the window
spun a chair under the smoke detector
stood on it,
smothered.

        I flapped around like a big dumb bird
        and went silent
        watching.

 In often-memories
You come to mind
     We, in that room
     small fires no space to breathe.

GE

Yesterday,
a man I had only just met
        -last name: Hassan-
and his assistant
          -a Scottish woman near retirement-
stuck a cold piece of metal the size of a modest carrot
up me
with no warning
        (though I had a good idea of what to expect)
to examine my bowels.

She did warn me
when they were about to blow warm air in.

Lying on my left side
facing a stark white institutional wall,
I teared up,
clutching and biting the sterile smelling pillow
              groaning.

I nearly slapped them away
from my exposed rectum
but toughed it out.

I wanted to vomit when,
in front of these strangers,
I involuntarily filled their balloon.

It was just enough time to convince myself
it could actually be and might get worse.
Then they withdrew their instruments.
I lay on my side
saying "I'm sorry. I'm sorry." over and over
as the nurse...

she says she has a son
who lives in Delaware
married an American girl
who was born on the exact same day of the same year as him
they met online, have kids
    --What are you studying?
    -I write poetry.
    --I'll just clean your bottom for you...

Incessantly apologizing
as someone's grandmother wiped
me in the fetal position feeling queasy wiping tears from my face.

They gave me a minute to collect my thoughts
and pull my pants up.
I shuffled to a chair across the room.
They scheduled a colonoscopy.
I walked uneasy to the waiting room
hoping the impatients sitting and restless wouldn't notice
my wet, sober eyes.

*

shells
(to Abd)

The lowest and most dejected thing of fortune,
Stands still in esperance, lives not in fear.

For several monotonous weeks
no words seemed to suffice
as worthy expressions
of all the things we'd worked so hard to learn.

The tedium of the mechanics of daily living
firmly settled in our psyches.
Faulkner, you said, called our days
successions of light and dark.
We discussed the uncertainty of our futures
worried sick about the present, our lack of creativity.
You, reclined in a chair, me pacing,
waiting for the floodgates to open
continually disappointing ourselves
with our own averageness.
The words weren't coming that dry summer.
We were in the midst of a drought.
It hadn't rained in weeks.

Then one afternoon it rained good and hard.
I watched drops thick as egg yokes
sploshing on the window
          ...Just stood there
feeling the water splash up from the sill.

We took a walk along the river
during a break in the rain.
I remarked how we needed this downpour.
We talked about Stevens and Joyce
the monolith of Modernism
the anxiety of influence.

Then we saw a snail on the path
and in danger of being trampled.
We tried to pick it up but it stuck, miraculously, to the ground
so much stronger than we thought a snail could be.
We used a stick and a rock
removed some dirt
the snail let go
we moved it to the grass when
another snail

and another
and another and still more
and slugs
and more and more snails

There must have been thousands of them.

Like children playing scientist,
we crouched and examined,
hypothesized, observed.
They must live in colonies, you posed.
We saw tiny snails, smaller than a fingernail.
Bigger more green ones.
There was one snail, swirly-backed
a lovely black and yellow striped shell
it stood out in the wet grass and was beautiful
and much prettier than the rest so we called her the queen.
The slugs were brown-almost-black
or near transparent milky yellow
slow, lazy, ugly...
Yes, I said, that is where the word sluggish comes from.

The snails went about their business
enjoying the wet earth.

They do not, each tiny snail, put the universe into perspective
                    proclaiming itself as the indisputable center.

Snails do not convince themselves they suffer.
They know the value of a good, hard rain.

We returned home reluctantly,
breathing the new air,
sliding along the dirt trail
the rain bringing us out of our shells
inspiring these first words I'd written in weeks.

Robin Marchal

Cottage Cat

In this Essex cottage,
Raised on yellow stocks of Victoria's reign,
Family succeeded family over generations.
In this room,
On pitted boards of cottage pine
They warmed together the flame blackened hearth.

And,   there, centred...

In the cries of children,
        Kindly sharing her decade of family space,
The black cat ruled with contentment.
In this room
        On her mat of coloured rags
They fought to stroke and cuddle her.

Until, she lay, at last, for luck, beneath...

In the wars of century,
        They bloodied the earth of alien parts
And returned, to toiling sweat in life's giving fields.
In this room
On sunlit evening and dark black morning
They centred the hearthbeat of their life.

And there, later, still, beneath...

In this Essex cottage,
        Today, decay demands renewal
Of worm powdered pine and damp black hearth.
In this room
        Sense of family past is wrenching
To the squeal of nails and splintering timber.

But there, beneath ...

In its foundations
        Lying on the comforting clay of home
The lucky black cat of continuity lives on.
In this room
        Her ageless bones emit continued life
And, my staring morbidity expands to smiling eternity.
And tomorrow, she'll be there, still, beneath...

*

The spiritual re-birth of Pioneer CK18, 2003

Standing, I see the heavy white painted decorated ceiling creamed yellow through decades of rising smoke. Standing, I hear whistled chatter through thin brittle stems of clay pipes, clenched in worn teeth flashing in hues of yellow and black. Outside, Turner and Whistler had painted the cold Thames of Wapping as it lapped the skirt of the 'Prospect of Whitby,' but inside with a fire in the grate, two men grouse behind pints of amber-dark Youngs ale.

"F'ing oysters again! That's all I eat. F'ing oysters!

"Bluepoints or Portuguese?"

"Eh? Never any dough for bread! Three times a week, every week, f'ing oysters! Wife's in service and that's what they give her to bring home. Oysters. But now they can't give them to her more than three times a week. That's the law! They make her sick too."

"Smacks bring 'em don't the? Brightlingsea. "

"Smacks? That's what you'll get if you mention that word again!"

"'Pioneer'. Sea oysters. Frisian."

"Frisian? Them's cows."

"Nah. Cowes is Portsmouth. Isle of Wight. I'm talking oysters from the Frisian Islands! Dredged. Put in flood pits. Back to Brightlingsea, then Wivenhoe. Train to Billingsgate. The get bought and the toffs feed 'em to us peasants. Governors gives 'em to everyone. Cheap. Lots of 'em. Scum food. Not cultivated. Bottom eaters. Filter water don't the. Eat anything."

"No wonder my gut's stewed with cramps. How do you know?"

"Couldn't stick it could I! So I've come to Wapping. Work the colliers. Steam, not sail. Easier. Tyneside, Whitby, here then back. They moor outside this pub. Along Wapping don't the?"

" Where you from then?"

"Worked on 'em didn't I. Until a month ago. A big smack. Skillingers they called them. 'Pioneer'. Sixty four feet long stem to stern. Crew of six. In winter, away for twelve days at a stretch but with weather, well it can be weeks. Dredge 50,000 oysters at sixty fathoms, hoist 'em day after f'ing day, shove 'em into the water pit; three hours sleep, mug of coffee, then trail and hoist day after f'ing day! Then, last month..."

"Yeah?"

"Last month. January, 1891..."

"Well?"

"Terschelling, West Frisian. Bitter cold wannit, no wind, then storms, men sicking up, the smell, f'ing oysters. Oysters, f'ing oysters rolling side to side in the pit, grating like a million pebbles, from side to side. Faster and faster, rocking side to side! 'Pioneer' was tossing, lurching, rise and fall, rain lashing, struggling to get the main down, sheets flying, out of control, skipper screaming but we couldn't hear him, we were awash and then gone, wan he. Man overboard. There, then gone wan he. The 'Gemini' and the 'Glance' went down as well – all hands. I was nearly sick. I've never been sick."

"So you've come back east..."

"Yeah. From the east. Brightlingsea, Colchester, couldn't stick it could I. Me dad's there, me grandad's there. Sea and ships, sea and ships, mud pie, building ships so sods like us can go and drown in Frisian weather. "

"It was a job though."

"I could build smacks. Cut all the oak and elm don't the. Ribs sawn to shape with the grain. Steam green oak planks, one and three quarter inches thick and shape 'em for the beams. All them trees. Hundreds of years to grow, then the rot in thirty. Wet and dry, wet and dry and the crew – always wet. Me dad, me grandad always wet! Colliers. I'll get work on colliers."

"I work colliers. No work."

"Oh. Yeah. I bet the old queen doesn't eat oysters.

"Queen Vic? She's dead. No-one ever sees her.

"Maybe somebody slipped her an oyster! She was all right.
'Pioneer'. Brave. Solid. Should keep it as a souvenir for the geezer
who drowned off her. Terschelling."

"Yeah. Got tuppence for another ale?"

"Yeah. Get two. Here's thruppence."

Smiling, I walk along the quay towards the reconstructed ketch
rigged, clinker smack, Pioneer CK18. She's moored, broadside on
to a surprisingly blue, slow, insidious tide shimmering away from
Brightlingsea to the River Colne. Most of her red brown, six foot
draught is below water but the plimsoll line, stretching its sixty four
foot length, is precise and cleanly edged by thick black paint. Above,
her superstructure, recently painted I'm told and therefore no access,
is fully covered. Her upper sides are draped shawl-like with heavy,
holly-green tarpaulin permitting only sight of twin, clear varnished
masts. The main, with her robust cross spreader, is secured fore and
aft by stays and shrouds. It rises thirty feet into the afternoon sun of
a blue sky.

I rejoice that The Pioneer Sailing Trust in 2003 encouraged
the re-birth of this fully formed foetus leading it to breaking waters
and giving it a life of its own. So many slaved and died in turbulent
conditions in the far off Frisian Islands, but then so many survived
– even in the Prospect of Whitby in Wapping, because oysters
formed a part of their staple diet.

The big smack whose first incarnation in upstream Rowhedge
in 1864, reclaimed by mud off West Mersea in 1942, gave spirit to
a new enterprise in 1998 which today offers opportunity to another
generation of young people to re-live in thought and practice an
emotional and physical past upon the high seas.

Petra McQueen

Instruction for a Smonnet[1]

1. A smonnet must have at least one smeader[2].

2. There must be fourteen episodes in a smonnet (Any more
    or less would not make a smonnet and would be classed as
    a sequence of smells).

3. In a Shakespearian smonnet each odour must be sniffed for
    6 seconds, or in a series of ten small sniffs. In a Petrachan smonnet
    the long sniff may be extended by a second and twelve small sniffs
    can be taken. Modern smonnets can have any number of sniffs.

4. A smonnet is still classified as a smonnet no matter how long
    or short the sniffs are.

5. A proviso to the above however is that some actual sniffing
    must take place[3].

6. The smace[4] must be as odour free as possible. If the smell of the
    smace is part of the smonnet then this must be classed as one or
    more of the fourteen smells (see 2.).

7. A barely perceptible smell[5] is acceptable for use within the
    smonnet. However, if the smeader is unaware that they have
    participated in the smonnet then it is understood that no
    smonnet or only part of a smonnet has taken place.

8. Smells may be repeated if desired.

---

1   A smell sonnet.
2   A smell sonnet reader.
3   After much controversy at the 2009 Munich Smonnet, Smillanelles and
    Smhiaku Conference, Hadley Burbeck's Necrofeelya was deemed not to
    be a smonnet because it was felt that the corpses used did not constitute
    smeaders.
4   Previously known as 'the area where the smonnet takes place'.
5   Often known as 'fresh air'.

9. Smonnets that turn, for example, bitter to sweet and vice versa, are often perceived to be the best. Modern smeaders and smoets[6] may disagree. A smonnet can still be classified as a smonnet without a turn present.

10. Natural smells are often believed to be preferable to synthetic smells. However, many modern smoets are now challenging that view.

11. Ammonium Carbonate (smelling salts) must be used sparingly if at all.

12. The use of Amyl Nitrate (poppers) is not recommended

13. Smoets are advised to seek permission from the relevant authorities before staging a smonnet. Insurance is available from the New Smonnet Society.[7]

---

6 A smell sonnet poet.
7 Previously known as The Sonnet Society. Please write to 19 Paget Road, Wivenhoe, Colchester, CO7 9JL. Fred Buck is no longer available at the above address and can be contacted via The Society for the Preservation of Smonnets. www.smonnetsisassmonnetswere.moonfruit.com.

No title

Against all good reason
I am searching for darkness
but cannot find it.
Outside, the town casts its orange glow.
And in my bedroom, lights off, curtains drawn,
my laptop winks and the day's sun seeps from
a white band on my trainers.
I close my eyes.
But see red and blue, then images brighter than life
As I slip into sleep.

Out, near the river, under a bridge of hawthorn,
I finally find it.
I discover that the darkness of the night is not empty.
In it are beasts and madmen
and the thick dank smell of the Hythe.
This was not what I thought I knew.
Not the darkness I seek.

So I look again. Carefully.
Wary of myself. I have nearly found it.
The darkness I think I know.
Perhaps I've been calling it the wrong name.
Misunderstanding it.
For, I think, it's in the white between the words of a page,
in the lull of a conversation,
the spaces between the drip of the tap,
and in that moment just before we touch.

Martin Reed

The Cat and the Clock

One midnight the clock abruptly woke the cat up, and this started an argument. The cat wailed loudly, remonstrating with the clock. The clock replied, "Hah! you are only a guest in this house, the humans no longer need your services, they only keep you around out of sentiment!" To which the cat answered, stiff-backed and haughty "I was a companion of humans before you were ever thought of, and will still be, when they no longer think of you!" At this the clock had nothing to say, except to tick sullenly, all night, and on into the next day.

*

The Dragon and the Horse

A dragon once stopped to ask directions of a horse he was passing. "Horse!" he called, "please tell me how I get to the high hall on the hill, how far is it? Hurry, for I am in haste - horse" But the horse did not reply, for the dragon, in his extreme haste, blinded by his own fiery emanations, had forgotten to avert his head when speaking to the horse; and the horse - had been burnt to a crisp.

Remember where you are.

Me, my Bath, and the Moth

I was having a good hot soak when a moth flew in and proceeded to be tortured to death by the hot water. I watched and thought about composing a haiku on the subject. Miraculously though the moth managed to struggle on to the dry land of my knee, where it crouched, staring. And suddenly I had a startling flash vision, of the huge hatred this creature had for me, the enormous maw it would have consigned me to, if it could. Which was a pity, really, because such a vision cannot at all be fitted into the vehicle of a haiku. So I brushed the moth onto the bathroom floor, where it dried itself, recovered, and in an incredibly cliched move - flew straight into a light bulb.

The Daddy-Long-Legs

Some people are scared of them. These creatures who spend most of their life as a very large yellow maggoty thing in the earth (called a leatherjacket) - five years or more, eating the roots of growing plants. After that they have just the one day as a daddy long legs, and on this last day they can fly, have sex, but can't eat (no mouth parts). Now what's so scary about that?

Gabriela Silva-Rivero

Out of the Cocoon

The butterfly flew straight at her, either attracted by the spring in the colours of her shirt or by pure coincidence. She arched her stomach inward and gave a skip back, an instinct that awakens in every living being when a small unidentifiable object hovers close; but the butterfly perched on her anyway.

It was a solid, black thing, Lepidoptera Lycaenidae Neozephyrusquercus, a Common Copper, she would say. It shone under the sun, with large pink eyespots in each of its lower wings.

She looked down at the wings, covered in brilliant dust-sprinkled scales. They were new and free of rents and bites, this specimen had probably just emerged from its cocoon. The thin antennae twitching in the wind, the miniature hooked legs that clung to her shirt. Its proboscis was rolled up and hidden under its head and she wondered if it had been used at all so far, or whether this butterfly was far too young to have ever eaten yet. Was it hungry after its long rest and metamorphosis inside its cocoon? Or was it too busy discovering the freedom of wings to bother?

No time to ask it, even as a whim. The butterfly was gone, immediately lost in the shadows of the garden. One last memory came to her mind then, fluttering, and for an instant she liked it too much to let go.

*

Two interns were waiting outside the reserve, talking to each other, and a wave of paranoia assaulted her immediately. She dismissed it just as quickly: gossip had followed her around lately, but she didn't wish to start doubting herself around the students.

'Hello, Melissa,' greeted one. 'Hot this year, isn't it?'

'Too much for March,' she agreed.

The second intern, a young woman, made a grimace. 'Seriously! Some nights I can't even get to sleep, I wake up in a pool of sweat.'

Melissa nodded. The same was happening to her lately, though she had never before been afflicted by nightly hot flashes. But then, she had never been hounded by gossip and she had never been cheated on. There was a first time for everything. And now every night the bed sheets seemed to mould to her body and constrict her, or she would wake up scared because she couldn't move her arms. It mystified her that the man next to her never noticed this and carried on sleeping while she tried to fight the heat.

'On the bright side,' insisted the first man. 'It means early hatchings. Did you see any babies, Melissa?'

'For sure. One of them landed on me, even.'

'Really? One of the Admirals?'

'A Copper, I think. Completely black, beautiful!'

'Oh, you've heard about the legend, about black butterflies, then?' he laughed. 'Supposedly, when a black butterfly lands on you, it's a sign you're gonna die soon.'

Melissa raised an eyebrow and told him not to be superstitious. They were all scientists, weren't they?

But, in truth, that was the last thing she had thought as the insect left her. The idea had fluttered into her mind, momentary but clear. Like all superstitions do in a scientific brain, like butterflies as they run from the sun.

*

Damien was waiting for her when she returned, reading a magazine with the television on.

'Hey,' he greeted her.

'Hey,' she answered and flew into the washroom.

She had the feeling that if she stayed in the room for any longer they would talk about the weather. Or about their jobs. But didn't they talk about that before, when they were still doing alright? The weather, the news, their jobs, politics, their families. Their relationship had been built on banal chatter as much as deep discussions about life and love.

But now she felt locked up, whatever is it they tried to talk. The words felt strained and the conversation fake – or perhaps this was only her own paranoia, which she was sure she had turned off but secretly thrived inside.

She was intelligent enough to recognize this was a punishment she was doling out to both of them. Damien had been ready to move out after she had caught him cheating, but she had begged him to stay. Life without him, she had said, wasn't something she could imagine at the moment, she didn't want to return every evening to an empty flat. She would give him another chance, she had said, and hadn't allowed him to say whether he was interested in that second chance at all.

But then what right did he have to be out and about, breathing wide and running deep while she couldn't dream, and the sheets coiled around her and solidified and stuck her limbs to her body?

Some nights it seemed like he truly wanted to make amends (or did he just want to pacify her, so that next time he tried to move out she would have no reason to deny him his right?), and then they would have dinner, watch a movie and try to make love.

*

The butterfly visited again the following week, perching on her writing board this time. Melissa refused to believe it could be the same one – what were the odds, after all, that in the whole of the sanctuary the same little insect would find her? What were the odds it would beat its own natural fear and approach her?

But there it was, black and shining and still very new, with its two pink dots in the hind wings.

The night before they had tried to have sex; but she had remained dry during the foreplay and he had remained limp. In an effort to hide her own unwillingness, she had tried to wake him up with her mouth, but it had been useless. They had gone to sleep, and again the heat had suffocated her throughout her dreams.

Melissa thought of herself as very much a scientist, lived her life through cause and effect. One thing had to necessarily cause another: nothing could be found to exist on its own. Studying had caused good grades and a good job. Eating healthily had made her lose some pounds, and if she could exercise she would lose even more. Hard work and proficiency had made her head of department even at a young age. And keeping youthful, flirty and sexually active should have led to keeping Damien; only it didn't.

The butterfly, who visited her for the second time against all possibilities, was either a cause for an effect that was yet to happen or a completely random factor in her life. It was a reflection of her own self or a reflection of love.

The butterfly's tongue wasn't retracted this time: perhaps it had just eaten. Both absorbed and diverted, she mentally repositioned the insect away from her, and then changed its meaning. She saw it lapping sugar from a flower; re-imagined it as something alluring, licking not something but someone: less of a basic instinct born out of need and more of leisure, developed for pleasure, for love.

But he hadn't reacted when she tried to take him into her mouth.

How many species of butterflies remain loyal to a particular flower species? She had read the number somewhere, not long ago, but couldn't quite remember. Even as they starved, even if other species were closer and were easier to access or carried more nectar.

She was re-inventing herself as a butterfly, becoming frail and dependent even when other sources of food were available without absorbing any of the strength the insect displayed to break out of its cocoon.

'So maybe you are going to die,' said the intern behind her, and the butterfly took off immediately.

'Hmm. Maybe. Or maybe it's just coincidence.'

'Hadn't you once said coincidence is the same as superstition?'

Yes, thought Melissa, but that was before Damien had cheated, and now life seemed more open to chance.

Instead, she said, 'Yes, but you were the one who invoked a superstition first. I'm not going to die because a black butterfly landed on me.'

'Twice.'

'And here I am, still alive.'

*

When she tried to kiss him, he turned away.

'Melissa, what am I even here for?'

'How do you mean?'

'This isn't – we aren't working things out, are we?'

'Why would you say that?'

'Because it's the truth!' his hands were quivering. He had dropped out of college to work as a chef, and had always claimed to be agnostic: unlike her, who lived from one scientific belief to another, he was deeply entrenched in his own accepted inability to know, and once mocked her need for a cause for every aspect of her life.

 Only now there was one single certainty in his life: he had no reason to be with her anymore. They weren't functioning anymore as a couple, or as individuals. They weren't "not working things out", they were just not working. And part of this was a role inversion: he was beginning to understand that his cheating was not the cause of their failing relationship, but the effect.

But she wasn't ready to forgive.

'We just need some more time,' she insisted, and that much wasn't a lie. She just wasn't sure what she needed time for.

She dreamed of herself divided in innumerable small shapes, each identical to the other and each processing a different part of herself, until the whole of her had been refined into something very small and fine, sitting strong in the palm of her hand.

*

Even if many more had hatched during the two past weeks, the butterfly didn't seem to have any trouble finding her, and she wasn't surprised to receive it either. Lacking any other perch, she offered a finger, and there the insect set. Three weeks had passed since it had first flown at her, and its wings were no longer as reflective, and its antennae were covered in dust.

But this time, she only looked at its eyes.

She had missed them before, in her first examination, the two compound eyes she had dreamed about. Hexagon over hexagon, as two small computers divided into thousands of diminutive processing units, all looking at her; refracting and reflecting her silhouette until it wasn't her anymore, but something strangely black.

When the butterfly fluttered again, she knew she was truly going to die, but she also remembered that butterflies die at least once before coming into their true shape.

*

Her eyes felt blurry that night. Naked in the bathroom, looking into the mirror, she couldn't quite make out her own form. Her hair was ragged and dark after the day and it grew like a shadow; extending towards her sides and framing her torso like millions of scales and advancing over her skin until her nipples became the eyespots in the lower wings.

Already the butterfly began to superimpose.

*

Sweat and moisture pooled all around her that night, more than any previous night, dripping from her nape, from underneath her breasts and over her legs. Her nightshirt solidified and stuck to her body, and the sheets followed, coiled around and too heavy to be comfortable. All through her sleep she felt her muscles aching, as though they had been immobilized for a long stretch of time, stuck in the same position.

There were no dreams of butterflies this time. There were only abstract feelings of hunger first, or perhaps a wild thirst that she could only understand as an empty stomach. In her dream, it occupied the whole of her and then transformed into a sense of strength that woke her up.

When she opened her eyes, light was beginning its crawl through the window shutters.

She broke through the heavy layer of covers, head first, then an arm and the other following, until she was uncovered and taking in the air. She peeled off her nightshirt and stretched, nude and clammy, out of the cocoon. Next to her, Damien slept undisturbed by the cold air that wafted over him. They had argued again before sleeping, but she held no memory of it. It had been lost in the mirror.

The blankets eddied around her calves as she hovered over the man, toes bent and ankles high. She felt her body eroding with every movement, becoming smaller and weightless and soft, and still felt the hunger that had been born in her dream. The black hair between her legs grazed the fabric of his pants, and her hands hooked them down.

Slowly he came to life – like a flower displaying itself, pistil, calyx and filaments, all. He woke up then, with a series of bleary grunts, hands flailing about, maybe trying to find her – to wave her away or to take hold of her, as he used to before?

But she alighted over him and lapped at his skin, taking in his moisture. There were mutters, somewhere above; something about her moving, using her hands, taking him in. But what need has the butterfly to listen to the flower? She was no longer tied, and would no longer make him think he was tied too.

He came in her mouth with a heavy grunt and a series of moans that she didn't quite understand nor cared too much about. Instead she got up and yanked shutters and windows open – the morning sun stripped the cold sweat away. Arms wide behind her, her silhouette cutting a pair of wings in the shadow that fell on the floor. With a flutter she slipped into the wind and into the light that warmed the spring into summer.

Jeremy Solnick

G-String

Get going goths gob grapes grow guttural groans gape getup google grope groupie gobble grapple gimmie good gander gamble gob-smacked gobble-de-gook gobstopper geeesie-em give generously genial gumshoe gleeful goliath grips gorgeous George gripe gorge gourd glow gravy gust ginger guitar guarantes gonorrhoea general grange gland gimlet genuflect gauze grenade grease gizzard govern gaze garnish gosh galosh gotcha grave gmdrop gloomy guarantee grimace glottal gotta getta goat gash Gethsemane gunner gnu gasp gestation genuine gander garnish glamorus green goddess groom gently grunt Geronimo gauge gangrenous git garb grammar grab gamma-globulin geriatric goose gerund gerontocracy generation game germane gigabyte gimbal glacial glittering German ganja gink gruesme gonk gong go-slow grow graceful groom gerrymander gargantuan gouge gossamer grumble growl gnomon goblin grand gargle goon Goodie gamete grune gizmo generator glorious glum goner gloop Galapagos Graham garden gadget grieve gramophone gopher grime ghastly gastronome gi guest gestate gossip gaseous gooseberry giraffe gingivitis grumpy Getafix grandfather grid gristle Gollum Guardian grub guessghostly grist giggle gubernatorial garbage

The Ballad of the Black Toad

Oh take the long forgotten path
to the end of the winding road
You'll find a sign that directs you
To the Gorge of the Black Toad

In a tower in Andalusia
There lived a cruel king
Whose evil ways came to an end
Of which poets still sing

The King decreed a thousand steps
be cut to the gorge below
So he and all his courtiers
Could watch the river flow

Oh no-one knows how many fell
Carving that steep hill side
Their bodies lie in the river bank
And only the river birds cried

There came a man out of the West
In rags and a long beard
Who said to all those slaving men
This king must not be feared

Lay down your tools you weary men
And listen to my song
For I come from a promised land
Where slavery is wrong

They bought the man before the King
He stood there proud and strong
'Bow down, bow down, you arrogant fellow
Or you will not live for long'

'Oh no, Oh no, I'll not do so
To no-one living or dead
No, not to emperor, king or clown
Do I kneel or bow my head'

The king frowned and his red guards ran
With upraised swords and staffs
'Cut out the tongue of that arrogant man
His body will feel my wrath'

He slipped right through their hands like dew
His rags fell to the floor
From out his mouth a white dove flew
And he was seen no more

In the evening thunder came
Lightning flashed on high
The King's great tower burst into flame
The smoke reached to the sky

Then from the Tower's highest step
The desperate king he leaped
And from his shattered body
a slimy black toad crept

Now on the spot where that tower stood
The tourists come and go
And buses park where gardens were
In Andalusia long ago
But if you take the forgotten path
At the end of the winding road
You'll find a sign that directs you
To the Gorge of the Black Toad

The Savage God

Shabbat in my sister's house
I scrutinise your artefacts
hanging on her walls

Carefully brushing away strata
From your runic figures and blueprints
Searching for a cipher in your midden

You were tied to the mast
Always listening to singing
Our ears were stopped with wax

You were High Priest
At some secret rite
We were not party to

Then you invoked the Savage God
Who took your beating heart
As you stepped out into the fiery mouths of dawn

On our lamp glass
You left an indelible smear
Of moth

Nine ways of looking at the death of Rattray

They sprouted ragged and snot nosed
in dusty townships.
They scrambled for stompies
while his kids went to school..
They did not get necklaced.
They slept with dogs
In corrugated iron shacks

He spirited me away
He summoned the dead for me
from their rest on the Mountain
He thrust an ox hide war-shield Into my hand
I ran barefooted with the impis through the veld
My ostrich feathers pluming in the sun.

Africa, your arachnid heart
dwells at the centre of our darkness
You leap out from behind your trapdoor
And devour the best of your offspring.
It is from our bleeding eyes
That your bitter rivers flow.

They stood sullen eyed before the Magistrate
claiming to have come as thieves
But they stole only his life.
As if the Angel of death had passed over
on leather wings and sent its dark seraphs
to slay Pharaoh's firstborn

Their anger broke upon him
as he crossed the drift.
It smashed his plus-foured
and pith helmeted body
onto the hungry rocks

Assegai - Zulu stabbing spear
Gogga - Insect
Impi - Zulu army fighting unit
Isandlwana - Battle at which Zulus defeated heavily armed British column
Necklace - of a burning car tyre
Stompies - cigarette butts
Tokolosh - evil spirit
Voetsek - Piss off

He said voetsek to the tsotsis
who leered from the compound fence.
He did not shudder at the Tokolosh
or listen for the scratch of its feet
in the night.

    They grew up hoarding
    milk cans and bottle tops
    They never spilled the water
    they carried from the standpipes
    but had no such feeling
    for the spilling of blood.

        He loved the goggas of the veld
        He loved the stories of soldiers
        more than the strategies of generals
        He loved the tongue of his Zulu brothers
        But he loved his own voice best
        And he loved to be called Baas.

Drunk from the slaughter at Isandlwana
they fell asleep on the Mountain
and missed their impi.
They awoke one and a half centuries later
their assegais still unslaked.

James Stannard

Ancarva

Standing, without shoes, on a rug
Tangle-patterned with ivy blossoms,
Before screen doors
Looking onto an eel-green marble balcony,

Ancarva and I watch the Camel Trail,
Sunsoaked gravel paths
Sinking into the armcrooks of half-waterless inlets,
Bicycle wheelspokes
Spitting, in light peppering shots, the same gravel
I flew onto shoulderblades first
At some forgotten time.

Coarse thatches of
Thistles, violets,
Snake over the uneven cobbled wall,
And run in curlicued paths down to the town,
The town with its clamour of emigrated
London haircuts, pearl necklaces and voices,

Rolled like dice from the hands of a doorway
Under the sign of a scudding swan,

And we scratch our sign on the contract,
And slide this town, this past,
Into our pockets.

Lectures in history

A seagull sweeps the
Purpling sky
As if on thermals
Of chattering crowds.

Below, its mirrored steel walls
Refract the stone library
And speared branches of half naked trees –
The building where I heard

Of trees called Daphne
Blooming under grasping, blistered fingers,
Of Candide's Odyssey of plagues
And pastries.

Where four years later,
I sat on hexagonal desks
Trying to find common ground
With future teachers,
Their heads riddled with Pythagorean theorems

And we discussed the advent
Of rebellious students who sniped
From behind glossy new books
Or took two weeks to become ghosts,

And now, sitting in a light chill,
One of my students in a fur-lined hood
Walks through those same doors
Toward metamorphoses and Satanic circles.

Tony Tackling

From Po/Me: Barking Odes

1

AM NOT making a grandigross STATEMENT OF POETIX—
     I'm more in the pome hell
 po/me frame of self where the po/me is a way to connect the self
portrait in a deathroom green with world outside and fuck the obj.
an ell equals ay equals enn equals gee equals etc. Though
 it maybe write it creates smug potes an tho Olson was a buffoon
(YOU WILL PAY
ATTENTION WHEN I'M SPEAKING AT YOU he shouted—
Herbie was juss looking at his watch, needed to catch a plain...
 am more in tune with self— It's like economics,
us making a system to use not the system usin us –
 So that big war between the linguine potes an the Olsonites
it was the po/me suffered as end product, result
 E.P. wrong too, nothing wrong with advertising soap,
people need cleaning, juss make the soap good,
 it'll moisturise forever/dedandruff your soul
your soul is a word I invented that means a hole host including
 your beauty in depth, questioning, EMPATHY
academics go what is beauty and I invented that word too and it means
things that make being alive more than just bearable
 I allow everyone to be their own judge of my ideas
but I allow myself to hate those who limit themselves when they're
educated enough
 to read those who ain't educated enough
I forgive but I don't see a way out of people losing limbs and I'm not
offering that to you, dear— The po/me needs to be written
about things other than the po/me and the po/me
takes care a itself it is ART creativity the religion
the bible   fiction and you use it to see things as long as you ain't
dumb cunt enough
 to have it use you to see things an langwitch gave birth
to us via the po/me we take control of langwitch so becoming the
only gods

we made god in our etc. The religion the self regulation
 understanding of form that is the only bastard form and all form
is a bastard wanting recognition
 from unacknowledged parents of us so
the practise of poetry is to practise your self

2

for duck toss involves the pillow
for the auld reality man in hiss (sic) bad
 you watch/weep willy cry
beneath blue covers and its sight
 glare silly strokes the pouring cat-a-ratz ~~
watching books spread INNER library
 (notes on pater's son
brown spine and the man mount'n body (
 St. Ructures maintaining structures of nada
  but the PO/me not the use
less the use of poetry
and the use of criticism and one pote
 has him tied on a chair –his books read to him
 he will be starved until he begs to die
with the paper cuts from his OWN SIN his name one
I. A. Richards
 and I wood Possum
wallpaper with the acceptance letters from
 to put it lightly SHITS –
                              there are one half shits
needing to count the STRESS OF THE CRIME
 winding relentless about my baby's wonder
and others who arsing language into language arsing ? art
 me in other half half-arsing \ wonder baby's stress
 nodding want relentlessly
port for   po/ME only
and at the point in   this pO/mE   I'd like to make it...

I um...er righter butt
 you non
plus am doing this –   emp
                         tearoom

3

coats seagulls plaque
slow / fast motion big board flowering
    (why not Cap'n Beefheart to organassized
two dollar room/broom
 when the general rolls it rules
radio broadcast/ bbc new
watch the willow branch towards
 ice burghers and Dave Att. grinning with
a check   a bomb
ecogomey gone for   pot
    today no different to yesterday or tomorrow
    the days of the week the same day and god does not rest nor do
    hotels or bastards`

 difference between now/then is rain
    no suits/ windows shutten
 shit squirrels borrowing
    come asteroid onto water terrorist
in all the big shows it dies afire
 and I want too
    have the flame viewable from the next room
 besides the slow ticker of shares
up/down turned arrows dribbling fiction
akin to wanking this mess what use
I say the mirror is hungover
)real words semblance
Murphy's musicMUSICMUSIC
    in head slush claw back
inscape they're horror creations of a SISTEREM inclusive of
papers where paper one half of which can be miscuntsrued
 to form effort straining one off
                       end

8

one mind wrap
 go wrong/right
WALL
more one than other blood
 patterning vessel on white wax dripping

from shooting ear down sights
got stuck on a train of
 for a few years – thought
too much on
RED RAILS AT SEVEN KINGS
 that external dissection
compartments rather than depart
ignored the last thing learned
 was the first spect of old sun
this is mess)()()(was a mess
 could kick your teeth out call it a sonata
gouge your eyes call it
 an experiment playing god with clay at Sadism
 let's reflect on what to do next no no
reflection but the reflex action
 WALL
don't believe in ghosts but
on the top floor is a mad man and there is nobody
 up there and afraid believe
 when asleep head steams
death appears/disappears/reappears or the dead do
the dead do do the dead do when awake
 the head steams
all over sudden

9

po/mE heavun
 like the work has a NO SENSE
skeleton project on the life
ending NOW
a choice occurs/blurs beginning chapter
    (Mr. Higgs/ Higgs Bison
will become spect of EMOP
 shift) no grandigross <<<but a flag
the thing is a rough estimate of eyebrows mirror raised
a patronising kaleidoscope
 have always wanted to
of aim   of course   the acadumbics' belly
this for them for me not us
    I read somewhere something an insurance man said about a
book of poems being

drunkard (((there is NOTHING serious

  book of pooems
  a dumb thing
  does nothin for noone
  but snowmen

16

detective of the PO/me: thirst decried
 waaaall) he got much thad was wrong, criminal etc.

thought the fatso played on the violin/drained marshes for aggro kulture
)))tho he did) was better in the butcher window) hung
 AVARICE – greed's fear in knickers
is way too much not too enough butt
knife of fascism in the hands of Laurel and Hardy hardly
 entertaining porspeck heart of capitalism not dead
as it exists in all our hearts – this is a statement on behalf of those
that escape – the ugly support a system that escapes
 them becomearseholewin

I am happy she said because I know Gawd loves me and though
 I know that is an impossibility I have become as tolerant
as the eel for jelly and perhaps I stopped caring
the gorgeous woman in leopard skin that talks of daughters
 understands empathy) what it means not is
she doesn't and never knows I mention her as a mussel
 outside its shell for her life I offer
this confusion
I am a tender lamb
soaked in phal

Kalyani Temmink

The Carousel

A moon eclipse, as the clouds blow out
out of my perfumed smile
A serenade, as the solar rays shine
shine into a glitter vile
A sparkle, as the luminous rain
rains through the shot glass
"pour me down, rise back up
    have one more, one's not enough"
Shrieking laughter, as the juggler plays
plays games with gas-lit reflections
A mirror image, of the face that holds
holds the stroke of the clock
"Now is the time, yesterday passed
   hold the kite, while summer lasts"
A whiff of grass, as the wind exhales
exhales through your polka-dotted lungs
A man in turquoise, and you wonder
wonder him to be or not
A stanza, as your eyes roll down
down towards the approaching end
"One more line, twenty-two's not enough"
    fill it up, leave it be!"
The one who'll read it   will be like me.

The Postcard

Crawling over the edge
Of a postcard from the desert -
A spider, limbs sprawled
Over a corner of sand
The plastic glazing:
Fingerprinted,
Discoloured,
Crumpled.

"Sunny rays send to you from me,
the absent one – lonesome in the space
Of the endless mustard horizon.
Hopes of bliss, security and safety
The wind waves to you the sun
a little postcard for my presence, a promise
not to leave you deserted – for too long."

The scent of heat as the postcard sways
through the letter box – into willing hands
The spider caught in the sealing of words
a token from a far away land

A smile at the sight
Of a postcard from the desert -
A spider, travelled across
the unknown sea:
Intact,
Crispy,
Dead – with a few last words

Sarah Jane Webster

Edge of Spring

Somewhere out there is a night where a man and a woman walk down a bright white path together to the Stour, boots crunching in crisp-topped snow. They pass under the crab apple tree they have admired through many seasons. She imagines the frozen, golden fruit underfoot. They enter a tunnel of stunted oaks. Beneath their snow blanketed canopies a dark carpet of crenulated leaves rolls down to Holbrook Creek. The hill to the left is drenched in moonlight and ridged in ice. Sloe bushes shudder, and shake off little shuffles of ice from their spiny black stems. In the future maybe, when she is stronger, she reaches for a branch. She wants to feel the temperature. Something. Is it thawing? No, it is still frozen, overloaded.

They reach the top of the hard and gasp at the scene in front of them. A curving avenue of glistening pods lines the route to the creek. The upturned tenders look as if they hold some alien life form awaiting orders to emerge from crystalline hibernation. Soon their feet are sinking in salty, part frozen water. She recalls the taste of salt and crushed ice on the edge of a cocktail glass in another lifetime, in Mexico. Huge chunks of ice, five or six feet across, are piled up like giant coins in a crazy game of arcade shove-halfpenny. He tells her that the freshwater running into the tidal creek has frozen and thawed, frozen again. The ice, dragged back and forth by the moonpull, has cracked and collapsed in on itself. Amongst the icy tectonic plates lie a tangle of little boats, one of them his, their jarred masts and spars glinting: brave hopes of summer immured in the heaving shards. The man and the woman reach for the frosted handrail of the small jetty, their woollen gloves sticking to rimed wood. Below the platform they can just hear water still running into the creek. The man tells her that they have borne enough in the last few years. He has decided that in the spring they will sail away. She senses something dark and threatening slide underneath the ice.

I am at the bottom of well. Keep head above water. Concentrate.
Do not want to go down anymore. Try to paddle. All I can do, just this.
Hold there. Everything impinges. So much noise. Just try and tune into
one sound. Narrow the focus. Tunnel so tight I can't move. Am stuck.

Is there someone up there, will they come? Think. Shout. Nothing comes out of mouth.

On the radio, the woman hears of another death. An old lady in a hospital died of starvation and dehydration. Nurses left her food and drink by the bed. They recorded that she did not touch it, then they took it away. They said no-one told them to feed her. The woman thinks, "No-one should need to be told to hold a cup or spoon to a frail old lady's lips." Yet the woman knows it is true and that you do not have to be old to suffer like this. Her brother almost died of a hospital infection after a routine operation. Two years later her father refused to go to the same hospital, even though his doctor had recommended urgent investigations for suspected cancer. He said he would rather stay at home undiagnosed and untreated. The day before he died the doctor called an ambulance. She was the one who said, "He doesn't have to go." She still feels responsible for his early death. Last year disappeared whilst she nursed her partner's mother. It felt like a penance but was not enough. She used to work for the NHS and inspired people to really care for their patients. She thinks that she should pull off the bandages from her tightly bound wounds and go to this work again. But she is too tired.

I was told depression was like a black cloud that came down and stopped you seeing the beauty, obscured the view. But it's not like that for me. I can see the beauty all right: a bright, piercing hell of beauty that I cannot reach. I am in a house with a huge picture window and no doors. Must find something to smash the window. A hammer, that's it, that's what I need. No. Have to sleep. In the morning... This morning will be different. Gather all energy, do not waste. Run if you can. Throw body at glass, again, again, again. Am in a tomb with glass sides.

She knew something was wrong that day on the river: a sharp January day, but with enough sun to give hope of spring. He was busy down below looking at charts, planning their great escape. She was on the tiller. Suddenly she was very scared. She tried to hold the fear in, told herself that she knew this stretch of the river, the depth sounder was on and there was little traffic. She took some deep breaths. Eventually, she found a voice to ask him to come up and take over. He wouldn't – said he was confident she could cope. She shouted, panicking out loud now. He shouted back, "Don't worry. You're officially competent crew." She shouted louder. He didn't respond. She could handle the boat. It wasn't that. She screamed.

A beautiful young man on the screen is lying in a van in Alaska, dying from eating bad seeds. He wanted to live off the land and learn its secrets, but thought he could do it alone. No-one to guide him. No-one to ask for help. The scenery is breathtaking. I wanted to watch the film but I know the end already and it is unbearable. It is a poison I can only take in small sips. It takes me days to watch it to the end. I am devastated. I wanted him to find a way across the water. He wanted to live. He was about the same age as my grown boys. Another day a tragic millionaire is going mad in a closed room filled with bottles of his own urine. I am shut in by my exhausted body. My partner talks and talks at me of the journey we will make when I am better but I know I have to try and shut him out. The world outside is bursting into life again and I am dying in here, watching TV.

The man makes her go outside. He wants a "proper" walk along the Orwell to Shotley Gate. She thinks she will not be strong enough to walk and asks if they can just drive down the cinder track to the creek. See if it has thawed. He refuses. Everything hurts. Even walking around the house grazes and bruises her. Ugly tiles, stair rails and carpets scrape her eyes, tear at her fingers and feet. She sees paintings and drawings, things she used to love, but feels they are as wretched here as she is. Now he is hauling her up a slippery bank to look at the barges sunk down in the mud. She tries to get some perspective. Perhaps she can walk it out. She heard someone did that once. She stumbles for an hour between marsh and farmland and asks if they can go back now. "A bit further," he says. All the while he copies the sounds of the seagulls, the curlews, the sandpipers, every dog he hears barking. Her head hurts – head hurts – head hurts - bird noise - tiny stabs of sound - in skull - incisions. She thinks she feels blood leaking out. She asks again to go back, to rest. He says if they just get to that headland over there they can cut across country. She thinks he may be trying to break her. Doesn't he realise she is already in pieces? They walk for another hour and he tells her, almost gaily, that he is on a see-saw and on one end is a packed bag. She is crying tired but something shifts in her. Perhaps he should go.

I am walking. He has just gone. I go towards the fishing lake and see the path ahead is strewn with old curled oak leaves. But the leaves turn out to be frogs - a dozen or more – completely still. Suddenly I have to stop too. I sit down amongst them. I think I may scare them, but cannot go on. I feel bludgeoned. I was trying so hard to come out of my depression, but he couldn't give me any more time. My fingers scrape into the dry dirt. I am clinging to the earth surface as if it is spinning too hard. If I don't hold on I could fall off. The frogs stay there. Their eyes stare blankly ahead.

She has always been the carer. She dreams of a young man who arrived at a hostel where she was working. He was so sad, slumped against a wall. She looked after him, brought him food and clothes. She wanted him to have a coat but could only find a dressing gown. No-one else seemed to realise how destitute he was. On waking she thinks of her sons, but realises it is she who is wretched. She still hasn't told them she is ill and on her own.

I look up at an old oak tree. Its limbs are like great enfolding arms – not yet leafed but ready to sprout from tiny knobbly buds - a live being. I want to touch its gnarled trunk. I lean against the tree and stretch my arms around the trunk, my face, suddenly streaming wet, pressed against the rough courses of the bark. I hear chiff-chaff, chiff-chaff and realise that birdsong doesn't hurt me today. I walk to the lake and watch the ducks chasing each other, scooping out V's of water.

Another day she makes a hollow in the grass by the lake. She sits here often now letting the sun warm her. She watches the waterlight dance on her legs. An oak leaf balances delicately on the skin of the water and moves very slowly across her vision. She reaches out, almost as if to a self she has mislaid a long time ago. She wonders if I can touch the water like the leaf, gently with my fingers, and not break the meniscus.

The phone vibrates in my rucksack. "Happy Mother's Day," my son says. I burst into tears and he asks, "What's wrong?" He thinks I may be anaemic as well as depressed and says that I should see a doctor. He will come next week and cook "properly" for me. In the meantime he jokes that I could learn to fish, illegally, in the lake. Surely, he says, there could be such a thing as therapeutic poaching? He offers to lend me his waders. I tell him I am afraid to go in the water.

A card arrives from her youngest son – he has painted an oak tree filled with paths of life. Today the sky is striped blue and white. Through the trees I glimpse a bright spinnaker harvesting the slight wind. I feel she is returning to me.

I have found a therapist, a large woman with an owl face. She says I remind her of that solid oak furniture signed in a hidden spot with a little carved mouse. For years I have been so strong for others, but

underneath I have been fearful, afraid to be my wild self. Each week we
wonder about the animal I might grow to be.

I sit on the sandy beach just past the Clamp House, enjoying the
spring sunshine, watching yachts leisurely sailing the Orwell.
The river undulates in beautiful syrupy sweeps towards me, gently
lapping along the seaweed strewn tide line. I stand up, take off
my shoes, and go to meet the incoming stream.

About the authors

Abdulhay Aborsan graduated with a BA in English Language and Literature from the University of Aleppo, Syria, in 2009. Currently, he is doing his MA in Creative Writing at the University of Essex. He is now writing his first novel, entitled *The Strangers of the Last Time*. Email *abd.lingua@gmail.com*.

Patricia Borlenghi studied at Reading and Bologna Universities before working in publishing for many years. She is the author of several children's books including: *From Albatross to Zoo*, *Chaucer the Cat*, *Dear Auntie* and *The Bloomsbury Nursery Treasury*. She is now writing her second adult novel, dividing her time between East Anglia and Italy. Email *patriciaborlenghi@gmail.com*.

Mark Brayley finished his MA in Creative Writing in 2010. He has written and performed poetry for many years and, following a passion for the work of OULIPO, curated an exhibition of visual poetry and conceptual art. Mark is currently writing the last few chapters of his first novel.

James Burch grew up in Croxley Green, a village on the outskirts of London. He has been a student at the University of Essex for the past four years but is now preparing to enter what the unimaginative refer to as the 'real' world. At present, James is hard at work on his first novel.

Cristina Burduja was born 1986 in the Republic of Moldova, and is absolutely obsessed with obsessions. Loves peeking through the keyholes of morgues, toilets, silent homes, mad houses and happy nests. She takes "killing" time literally and finds it very weird to write this biography in the third person. She. Who? Me. Oh! Her hole in the door: *cristinaburduja@yahoo.com*.

Steph Driver has a BSc in Natural Sciences and is now studying for an MA in Creative Writing. She is interested in combining computer science and creative writing through constrained writing and has developed a couple of small C# programs in order to construct her calligrams. Find out more at *www.stephdriver.co.uk*.

Lydia Graystone graduated with a BA in Creative Writing from Essex in 2011. She is currently an editorial intern working on a project about the BBC at openDemocracy. She spends her free time working on a young adult novel entitled *Minnesota Nice*. Email *lydia.graystone@gmail.com*.

Joshua R. Grocott has a BA in Creative Writing from the University of Essex and is now undertaking his MA in the same thing at the same place. When he isn't portraying pandas as people and people as pandas in his first novel, he's usually working as a freelance copyeditor or writing poetry with pictures in it. Find out more or less at *www.joshuagrocott.co.uk*.

Leanne Haynes has recently finished a PhD at the University of Essex, specialising in St. Lucian literature. She has a monthly online column with ARC, a publication that focuses on emerging artists from the Caribbean. Haynes has had poems and photographs published in the UK and the US.

Oliver King studied creative writing at UEA before beginning his MA at Essex. Living in Colchester with his wife and two children, he is currently working on a novel and hopes to one day write full-time.

Emma Kittle studied politics and economics at the University of Bath before training as a primary school teacher. She completed her MA in Creative Writing at the University of Essex in 2011. Currently working as a Reading Recovery teacher, she also hosts Colchester's community writing group, WriteNight. Email *emmakittlepey@hotmail.co.uk* or follow @ekittl on Twitter.

Matthew L. Kroll, an Indiana native, has also lived in Oregon, New York City and Essex, where he received MAs in Continental Philosophy ('05) and Creative Writing ('10). He is now a doctoral student in the Philosophy and Literature Program at Purdue University. His writing explores memory and place.

Robin Marchal trained in acting at the Webber Douglas Academy and has a BA Humanities from The Open University. He hopes a new two act play will help attain an MA in Theatre and is thrilled to have his short, *The Aspie Kid,* chosen for performance in Essex's Lakeside Theatre in June 2012. For more information visit *www.actorsandwriters.org*.

Petra McQueen is a writer, teacher and part time MA Creative Writing student. Although two novels and various short stories lie unloved and untouched in her desk drawer, she has been lucky enough to have pieces published by The Guardian, Cabinet des Fées, Leaf Fiction, Whidbey Writers' Prize, and Chapter One Publishers. She also writes biographies of famous writers for Collca Publishers: *www.collca.com/PetraMcQueen.*

Martin Reed is an ex computer scientist who now spends his time writing and performing (usually, he performs what he writes). He has an interest in the folk and myth-based literature which forms the imagal bedrock of western culture; he has an interest in breaking through this bedrock, to see what other formations might be possible. Email *voiceit2006@yahoo.co.uk.*

Gabriela Silva-Rivero was born in Mexico City in 1985. She is currently completing an MA in Creative Writing at the University of Essex. Her short stories have appeared in online magazine *Cuadrivio*, and her first novel, *Los doce sellos* (The Twelfth Seal) was published in 2009. She plans to alternate between England and Mexico and write in both languages.

Jeremy Solnick retired from his practice as a solicitor in 2007 and started a BA Honours degree at Birkbeck. He is currently on the MA Creative Writing course. Jeremy is interested in narrative poetry and in finding ways of adapting ancient mythologizing techniques to the retelling and interpretation of contemporary events.

James Stannard finished a BA and MA in Creative Writing at Essex, and is currently studying for a PhD in Literature and has been employed as a seminar teacher. His speciality is William Faulkner and Southern Literature, and his poetry is primarily influenced by Modernist and Post-modern works.

Tony Tackling is an Essex poet, currently completing a PhD at the University of Essex. His email address is *tonytackling@yahoo.com.*

Kalyani Temmink is a poet and short-story writer, currently an MA Creative writing student at the University of Essex. She is the creator and editor of the first edition of *The Essex Poetry Compendium*, co-editor of *Creel*, and has successfully managed the Poetry Project for two years, organizing evening poetry readings at the University.

Sally Jane Webster is an East Anglian writer and artist interested in walking, nature and wild therapy. She is writing a book on women and pilgrimage. A graduate of the University of Essex MA in Wild Writing: Literature and the Environment, she is studying for a doctorate in existential therapy and counselling psychology. Email *sallyhollyhock@hotmail.co.uk*.

Lightning Source UK Ltd.
Milton Keynes UK
UKOW051035161112

202307UK00003B/4/P